Climbing California's Fourteeners

Help Us Keep This Guide Up to Date

Every effort has been made by the author and editors to make this guide as accurate and useful as possible. However, many things can change after a guide is published—trails are rerouted, regulations change, techniques evolve, facilities come under new management, etc.

We appreciate hearing from you concerning your experiences with this guide and how you feel it could be improved and kept up to date. While we may not be able to respond to all comments and suggestions, we'll take them to heart and we'll also make certain to share them with the author. Please send your comments and suggestions to the following address:

FalconGuides
Reader Response/Editorial Department
246 Goose Lane, Suite 200
Guilford, CT 06437

Thanks for your input, and happy trails!

Climbing California's Fourteeners

Hiking the State's 15 Peaks Over 14,000 Feet

Toby Evans

FALCONGUIDES

GUILFORD, CONNECTICUT

FALCONGUIDES®

An imprint of Globe Pequot, the trade division of The Rowman & Littlefield Publishing Group, Inc.
4501 Forbes Blvd., Ste. 200
Lanham, MD 20706
Falcon.com

Falcon and FalconGuides are registered trademarks and Make Adventure Your Story is a trademark of The Rowman & Littlefield Publishing Group, Inc.

Distributed by NATIONAL BOOK NETWORK

Photos by Toby Evans unless otherwise noted
Maps by Melissa Baker

British Library Cataloguing-in-Publication Information available

Library of Congress Cataloging-in-Publication Data
Names: Evans, Toby, author.
Title: Climbing California's fourteeners : hiking the state's 15 peaks over 14,000 feet / Toby Evans.
Other titles: Climbing California's 14ers : hiking the state's fifteen peaks over fourteen thousand feet
Description: Guilford, Connecticut : FalconGuides, [2021] | Series: A Falcon guide | "Distributed by NATIONAL BOOK NETWORK"—T.p. verso. | Includes bibliographical references. | Summary: "Climbing California's Fourteeners informs adventurers about each of California's 15 mountains that top out at over 14,000 feet"— Provided by publisher.
Identifiers: LCCN 2021009760 (print) | LCCN 2021009761 (ebook) | ISBN 9781493045464 (Trade Paperback : acid-free paper) | ISBN 9781493045471 (ePub)
Subjects: LCSH: Mountaineering—California—Guidebooks. | Hiking—California—Guidebooks. | Trails—California—Guidebooks. | California—Guidebooks.
Classification: LCC GV199.42.C2 E93 2021 (print) | LCC GV199.42.C2 (ebook) | DDC 796.52209794—dc23
LC record available at https://lccn.loc.gov/2021009760
LC ebook record available at https://lccn.loc.gov/2021009761

One of my earliest memories of the backcountry and mountains came at a very young age. My mother, JoAnn, took my sister and me on a camping trip when I was nine or ten. She loaded up our 1973 Volkswagen Squareback and a little trailer and set out west to Yellowstone, the Tetons, and the Bitterroots—a single mom with two young kids camping their way through some of the prettiest areas of our country. She had discovered the beauty and wonders of the forest and mountains during college when, with a group of friends, weeks at a time were spent wandering through Mother Nature. On this trip, time was spent hiking through our national parks, cooking over a campfire, and listening to the sounds of the animals. To this day I cannot think of a better summer vacation. I fell in love with the backcountry right then and there. She raised us by herself and encouraged playing in the woods and exploring. Forty years later, she is unconditionally supportive of my love of the outdoors . . . after all, it *is* her fault in the first place.

Mom, thank you!

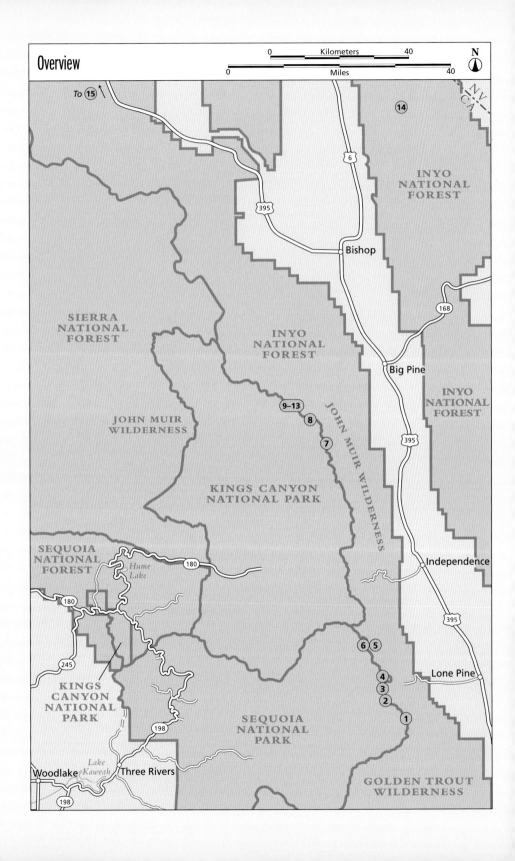

Overview

Kilometers
0   40
Miles
0   40

N

To 15

14

INYO
NATIONAL
FOREST

6

395

Bishop

168

SIERRA
NATIONAL
FOREST

INYO
NATIONAL
FOREST

Big Pine

INYO
NATIONAL
FOREST

JOHN MUIR
WILDERNESS

9–13

8

JOHN MUIR WILDERNESS

7

395

KINGS CANYON
NATIONAL PARK

SEQUOIA
NATIONAL
FOREST

Hume
Lake

180

Independence

180

395

245

KINGS
CANYON
NATIONAL
PARK

6 5

4

3

2

Lone Pine

198

SEQUOIA
NATIONAL
PARK

1

Woodlake

Lake
Kaweah

Three Rivers

GOLDEN TROUT
WILDERNESS

198

Contents

Foreword x
Introduction 1
    What Are the California Fourteeners? 1
    Get Your Permits 3
    When to Climb 7
    Do Not Go Alone, and Leave a Plan 8
    Leave No Trace 8
    What to Expect before Hitting the Trail 10
    Hydration! 11
    There Is Danger in the Hills 13
    Must-Have Gear 18
Map Legend 26

The Climbs

  1. Mount Langley 27
  2. Mount Muir 38
  3. Mount Whitney 58
  4. Mount Russell 76
  5. Mount Williamson 87
  6. Mount Tyndall 99
  7. Split Mountain 111
  8. Middle Palisade 120
  9. Thunderbolt Peak 133
10. Starlight Peak 143
11. North Palisade 150
12. Polemonium Peak 158
13. Mount Sill 166
14. White Mountain 174
15. Mount Shasta 185

Summiting the California Fourteeners: An Author's Retrospective 198
Terms and Definitions 206
References 211
About the Author 213

Foreword

1972. I climbed my first mountain at age 15 in the High Sierra. The experience of drinking from tiny streams in high meadows above timberline and scrambling from ledge to ledge to reach the rocky peak was like a vivid dream of wonderland. That day changed me and redirected my life. After graduation from high school, I drove to Lone Pine with a friend and we hiked and ran to the top of Mount Whitney, barely escaping being hit by lightning on our way down. That was my first 14er.

In the following years I got deeply into technical climbing, from hard scrappy routes at Joshua Tree to multiday ascents of big walls such as El Capitan in Yosemite. But the dream of being high in the lonesome, windswept starkness of the Sierra's amazing mountains remained the pinnacle of spiritual existence.

There is nothing on earth to compare with the deep, deep blue of the sky as seen from above 14,000 feet. There is no grass, no trees, no "green"—just grays, blues, blacks and whites, and a splattering of yellows and browns. The rocky mineral alien world up there overwhelms the senses and leaves one feeling both out of place and intimately connected at the same time.

It is that connectedness that stays with you. The adventure and the challenge draw you in, the effort and exhaustion create determination, and the final summit rewards with its views and validation, but it's the quiet thing that no one talks about, the quiet loneliness of the rock, the deep connectedness with earth and yourself and time—that's the thing that stays with you and draws you back again and again. It's that raw, primal connection with nature that you will remember when you are old, sitting in your rocking chair and trying to describe why you once climbed mountains.

So, go. Do it. It will change you.

Jack McBroom
Former speed record-holder of the California 14ers
November 2019

Introduction

This book was designed to introduce the beginning to moderately experienced individual to the tallest mountains in California. While each of the 15 mountains can be climbed in a variety of ways, only the primary, or classic, routes to each of the summits have been chosen for this book. The emphasis has been placed on helping the new climber reach each summit and return home safely. Before attempting to summit any of the mountains described in this book, the reader should have a reasonable fitness level and backcountry experience. The book starts with the easier and less technical trails and mountains that you can hike right to the summit and progresses to the more difficult peaks that require a higher skill set. By choosing to highlight the primary routes from trailhead to summit, the demand for route-finding skills has been minimized.

From trailhead to summit, each of the 15 peaks have been traversed, researched, and dissected by the author to help ensure your trip is successful. Step-by-step directions from the nearest town to the trailhead will get things started. From there the trail will be described in detail, including ideal camping spots, scenic vistas, and locations of fresh water. If special equipment, like crampons, is required on a mountain, this will be addressed. It is important to note that the author had moderate mountaineering experience prior to undertaking this project.

The intention of this book is not to be an instruction manual on general hiking, camping, or backcountry activities, nor is it intended to be a guide to technical climbing skills or equipment. These activities are hazardous, and it is the responsibility of the individual to learn proper techniques to ensure safety. Individuals should seek professional instruction to learn rope-climbing techniques before attempting to use them on a mountain. Please keep in mind that injuries can, and do, occur while climbing and hiking in the mountains. Experienced hikers and climbers have had to be rescued and evacuated from the backcountry. Injuries, and death, from falls, weather, lack of preparedness, and inattention are recorded in the California fourteeners every season.

What Are the California Fourteeners?

In California they stand tall against the stars and sky, vigilantly looking down on us. They tempt us to scale them and share in the vistas they showcase below. They are made of daunting ridgelines and conditions that, if not properly prepared for, can lead to injury or worse. At more than 14,000 feet above sea level, the 15 mountains that we call the California fourteeners (14ers) provide a physical and mental challenge that will push us to our limits. The allure of the summit and overcoming the many challenges drives more than 100,000 people to attempt to climb a fourteener each year.

Unlike the fourteeners in the rest of the United States, the California fourteeners are much less accessible and often require miles of hiking to reach their bases. While you can drive to within a few miles of many summits in Colorado, for example, the

1

majority of those in California will entail a round-trip of 18 to 26 miles. A brief history of each mountain is included in each specific chapter.

The vast majority of California's fourteeners can be found in the granite mountains of the Sierra Nevada mountain range. This includes the tallest mountain in the lower 48 states, Mount Whitney, which towers above the region at 14,505 feet above sea level. From the access near Lone Pine to the trailhead outside of Big Pine, the Sierra fourteeners look like this:

- Mount Langley, 14,025 feet, Class 1
- Mount Muir, 14,012 feet, Class 3
- Mount Whitney, 14,505 feet, Class 1
- Mount Russell, 14,088 feet, Class 3
- Mount Williamson, 14,375 feet, Class 3
- Mount Tyndall, 14,018 feet, Class 3
- Split Mountain, 14,058 feet, Class 2
- Middle Palisade, 14,108 feet, Class 3
- Starlight Peak, 14,220 feet, Class 4
- North Palisade, 14,242 feet, Class 4
- Polemonium Peak, 14,100 feet, Class 4
- Mount Sill, 14,153 feet, Class 4
- Thunderbolt Peak, 14,003 feet, Class 4

The remaining two fourteeners lie outside of the Sierras. To the east in the White Mountains is White Mountain, 14,252 feet, Class 1. Ten hours to the north in the Pacific Rim chain you will find a dormant volcano, Mount Shasta, 14,162 feet, Class 3.

Each of these mountains offers a unique climbing and hiking experience. This book has been designed to provide a plan to successfully reach the summits. The primary routes, including camping areas, locations of fresh water, and features specific to each mountain, will be laid out. It should be noted that this book does not cover all of the known routes, but rather serves as a guide for inexperienced to moderately experienced climbers venturing out for the first time. With time and preparation, reaching the summits can be a story shared for years to come.

To help explain the difficulty of an individual mountain, the Sierra Club created a class system used in the United States called the Yosemite Decimal System (YDS) to rate a hike, trail, or climbing route. Each of the 15 mountains discussed in this book has been assigned a class based on difficulty, and the book has been laid out from easiest to most difficult. Here are the YDS definitions:

Class 1: Walking with a low chance of injury. Hiking boots are a good idea.

Class 2: Simple scrambling, with the possibility of occasional use of the hands. Little potential danger is encountered. Hiking boots are highly recommended.

Class 3: Scrambling with increased exposure. Handholds are necessary. A rope should be available for learning climbers, or if you just choose to use one that day, but is usually not required. Falls could easily be fatal.

Class 4: Simple climbing, with exposure. A rope is often used. Natural protection can be easily found. Falls may well be fatal.

Class 5: Considered technical roped free (without hanging or pulling on the rope, or stepping on anchors) climbing; belaying and other protection hardware is used for safety. Un-roped falls can result in severe injury or death. Class 5 has a range of subclasses, ranging from 5.0 to 5.15d, to define progressively more difficult free moves.

Get Your Permits

Before hitting the trail you must have a permit to access the backcountry. These permits, issued by the National Forest Service (NFS), serve many purposes to ensure your safety and enjoyment during your time in the wilderness. Each permit essentially registers your itinerary with the Inyo National Forest. Mount Shasta, in the Shasta-Trinity National Forest, requires a permit as well. White Mountain can be hiked without a permit. The date and location of entry, camping locations (if necessary), and the date and point of exit along with the names and number of people in your group will be listed on the permit. Each member of your party needs to carry their permit at all times. Rangers will randomly spot-check permits.

Several options are available to obtain the permit you need. Many trailheads have self-serve kiosks where you can pay for a permit on the spot. The Recreation.gov website will allow you to apply for a permit, fill in the details, and pay for the permit in advance. Reserving your permit in advance of your trip will help ensure you get to climb on specific dates. This option will require you to pick up your permit in person at one of the following stations:

Eastern Sierra Interagency Visitor Center, junction of US 395 and CA 136, 2 miles south of Lone Pine; (760) 876-6200

White Mountain Ranger Station, 798 N. Main St., Bishop; (760) 873-2500

Mammoth Lakes Visitor Center, 2500 Main St., Mammoth Lakes; (760) 924-5500

Mono Basin Scenic Area Visitor Center, US 395 North, Lee Vining; (760) 647-3044

Walking up to the counter at any of these stations may allow you to get a permit that day on a first-come, first-served basis. This option can be risky, however, since a limited number of permits are available. If you can be flexible with your start date and location, the chance of being issued a permit in this fashion goes up. The NFS will begin issuing walk-in permits at 11:00 a.m. the day prior to entering the backcountry. Keep in mind that the increased demand on weekends and holidays may limit

INFORMATI

CASHIER

PERMITS

EXPLORE

Backcountry permits, maps, guidebooks, and up-to-date trail conditions can be picked up at the Eastern Sierra Interagency Visitor Center just outside of Lone Pine. The walk-up permit lottery takes place every morning for those last-minute plans.

your ability to obtain a permit. These options work for all but one of the fourteeners, Mount Whitney.

Mount Whitney, the tallest point in the lower 48 states, attracts more people annually than any other fourteener in California. With one of the most iconic approaches, including the 99 switchbacks, daily traffic on the Whitney Portal Trail is limited to 100 permits, including 60 overnight use, per day. Whitney permits must be picked up at the Eastern Sierra Interagency Visitor Center. The NFS holds an annual lottery for hiking and backpacking permits on the Whitney Portal Trail. Applications are accepted from February 1 through March 15. Any permits left over after the lottery is completed typically go on sale April 1 on a walk-up basis.

Mount Whitney Permit Lottery Process

All applications are held until after March 15. Applications are assigned a random order to be processed, and software checks if there is space for the dates you requested. Lottery application must be completed online at Recreation.gov (applications are not accepted by mail or fax). On the application you indicate:

- Date(s) you want to hike.
- If you want a day hike or overnight permit.
- Maximum to minimum group size.
- Alternate dates, up to 15 trip choices on one application.
- Names of three alternate leaders. Alternates cannot be changed or added later. Provide a valid email address for each alternate, as alternates must respond to email within 72 hours and accept responsibility.

Make sure all of your information is correct before you check out the cart. Applications cannot be changed or modified later. Submit your application by checking out the cart and paying the $6 application fee.

Lottery results are posted to your personal profile on Recreation.gov on March 24. If you won your date, decide how many people you want to keep before you accept. In April you must pay the $15 per-person reservation fee to claim your date. Once you have paid the reservation fee, there are no refunds.

Lottery Terms

Submit only one application. You may request up to 15 alternate dates on one application. Do not submit multiple applications. Groups that do submit multiple applications will be rejected. You are limited to win one trip from the lottery each year. If you want more trips, additional reservations can be made after the lottery. Unclaimed dates will be canceled and released for web reservations on May 1.

- Reservations are only valid for the stated entry date or permit type. No rain checks. No rescheduling.
- Groups larger than 15 people are prohibited.
- Reservations cannot be resold or transferred.

- Alternate leaders cannot be added or changed later.
- Only the leader (or verified alternate) listed on application can pick up or use the permit.

After the Lottery

On March 24 you can log on to see if your application was successful. Before you accept a date, decide how many people you want. If you accept a smaller group size, the space given up cannot be restored. Once you accept and pay, there are no refunds.

April 30 is the deadline to claim the date awarded. Log into your account on Recreation.gov and open the link to your lottery application. If you're not interested in using the awarded permit, you should decline. Dates cannot be transferred, rescheduled, traded, or sold. You cannot change the date, leader, or permit type. Only the awarded choice can be claimed.

To accept, you will need to complete the trip information and use the shopping cart to pay the $15 per-person reservation fee. Fees are final after checking out the cart. No refunds.

- Verify that the date, permit type, and group size are what you want.
- For overnight trips *longer than one night*, verify your exit date and exit trail. John Muir Trail hikers select their exit location to indicate the section they are hiking. You can reopen the reservation later (after April 30) to revise and fill in your full itinerary.
- You may reduce your group size and only pay for the number of people you choose to accept; however, space cannot be restored unless space becomes available later.

When to Climb

While many of the fourteeners can be summited during the winter months between December and March utilizing advanced techniques and skills, for the purposes of this book the climbing season will be from early spring to late fall. The snowpack in the Sierras averages in feet, not inches, and will, in spots, linger into early July. Snow covering talus fields, like the Williamson Bowl, can make travel over these areas much more pleasant. However, the use of crampons and ice axe will be required. The primary trails discussed in this book should be completely devoid of snow by mid-July.

During the summer months, popular camping spots and meadows attract mosquitoes and biting flies. Even though I climbed at several different times of the year doing the research for this book, I found that August and September were the most pleasant months in the Sierras. The daylight hours are long, and the weather is fairly predictable. When possible, time your trip to coincide with a full moon. The best time to climb will be during the dry season from July through October.

Do Not Go Alone, and Leave a Plan

If only for safety reasons, one should never venture into the backcountry alone. Taking a trip with a partner or small group provides safety and security in numbers should an emergency arise. The shared experience will make the time and effort more enjoyable as well. When choosing a hiking/climbing partner, look for someone with similar physical fitness and skill levels. Know that everyone moves at different speeds and establish a plan on how to handle those differences. It may be as simple as setting a goal destination for each day so that everyone in your party understands the expectations.

Depending on the mountain and time of year, you may see others on the trail. Mount Shasta and Mount Whitney, being the most popular of the fourteeners, will almost always have a high daily hiker count. Others like Split Mountain see only a fraction of the traffic.

A good rule of thumb is to create a detailed itinerary of your trip before you leave home. Include the dates you are traveling, the trailhead you will access the backcountry from, campsites, summit days, and when you should be expected to return to civilization. It would also be wise to include the make and model of the vehicle you are leaving at the trailhead. Leave this information, along with the phone number of the ranger station closest to where you will be (see the "Get Your Permits" section), with someone at home. You can also leave a copy of the itinerary in your car. This information can help narrow down a search area should an emergency arise.

Leave No Trace

The public lands in the United States are composed of national forests (administered by the NFS), national parks and monuments (National Park Service, or NPS), Bureau of Land Management (BLM) lands, and wilderness areas and belong to all of us. By adhering to the seven "Leave No Trace" principles, we help ensure that future generations can enjoy these natural resources. The principles are:

Plan Ahead and Prepare
- Know the regulations and special concerns for the area you'll visit.
- Prepare for extreme weather, hazards, and emergencies.
- Schedule your trip to avoid times of high use.
- Visit in small groups when possible. Consider splitting larger groups into smaller groups.
- Repackage food to minimize waste.
- Use a map and compass or GPS to eliminate the use of marking paint, building rock cairns, or flagging.

Travel and Camp on Durable Surfaces

- Durable surfaces include maintained trails and designated campsites, rock, gravel, sand, dry grasses, or snow.
- Protect riparian areas by camping at least 200 feet from lakes and streams.
- Good campsites are found, not made. Altering a site is not necessary.
- In popular areas:
    - Concentrate use on existing trails and campsites.
    - Walk single file in the middle of the trail, even when wet or muddy.
    - Keep campsites small. Focus activity in areas where vegetation is absent.
- In pristine areas:
    - Disperse use to prevent the creation of campsites and trails.
    - Avoid places where impacts are just beginning.

Dispose of Waste Properly

- Pack it in, pack it out. Inspect your campsite, food preparation areas, and rest areas for trash or spilled foods. Pack out all trash, leftover food, and litter.
- Utilize toilet facilities whenever possible. Otherwise, deposit solid human waste in catholes dug 6 to 8 inches deep, at least 200 feet from water, camp, and trails. Cover and disguise the cathole when finished.
- Pack out toilet paper and hygiene products.
- To wash yourself or your dishes, carry water 200 feet away from streams or lakes and use small amounts of biodegradable soap. Scatter strained dishwater.

Leave What You Find

- Preserve the past: examine, photograph, but do not touch cultural or historic structures and artifacts.
- Leave rocks, plants, and other natural objects as you find them.
- Avoid introducing or transporting nonnative species.
- Do not build structures or furniture or dig trenches.

Minimize Campfire Impacts

- Campfires can cause lasting impacts to the environment. Use a lightweight stove for cooking and enjoy a candle lantern for light.
- Where fires are permitted, use established fire rings and fire pans or build mound fires.
- Keep fires small. Only use downed and dead wood from the ground that can be broken by hand.
- Burn all wood and coals to ash, put out campfires completely, and then scatter cool ashes.

Respect Wildlife

- Observe wildlife from a distance. Do not follow or approach them.
- Never feed animals. Feeding wildlife damages their health, alters natural behaviors, habituates them to humans, and exposes them to predators and other dangers.
- Protect wildlife and your food by storing rations and trash securely.
- Control pets at all times, or leave them at home.
- Avoid wildlife during sensitive times: mating, nesting, raising young, or winter.

Be Considerate of Other Visitors

- Respect other visitors and protect the quality of their experience.
- Be courteous. Yield to other users on the trail.
- Step to the downhill side of the trail when encountering pack stock.
- Take breaks and camp away from trails and other visitors.
- Let nature's sounds prevail. Avoid loud voices and noises.

What to Expect before Hitting the Trail

To reach the summit of a California fourteener, the trailhead must be reached first. Reaching Bunny Flat (Mount Shasta), Cottonwood Lakes (Mount Langley), and Whitney Portal (Mount Muir, Mount Whitney, and Mount Russell) simply requires driving up a paved road. During winter months the length of the drive will vary depending on snow cover. To reach other trails such as Red Lake (Split Mountain) and Shepards Pass (Mount Williamson and Mount Tyndall), it is advisable to use a high-clearance vehicle.

Once your party has reached the trailhead, the uphill challenges begin. Depending on the mountain, the starting elevation will be between 6,500 and 10,000 feet and you will end up over 14,000! Plan on a round-trip distance from the car to the summit and back ranging from as few as 9 and, potentially, more than 28 miles depending on your route choices.

How long it will take depends on the speed at which you can move. According to Naismith's Rule, a person can cover 3 miles an hour on flat terrain and an additional hour should be added per 2,000 feet of elevation. Using this formula for Mount Whitney's 22-mile round-trip and 6,145 feet of elevation gain, a very fit person should be able to complete the hike in approximately 12 hours. This hike could take more than 24 hours, so prepare wisely. But do not forget to add in rest breaks, stopping for pictures/food, and trying to acclimate to a lower oxygen content than most of us are used to. It would not be uncommon for these activities to add another 4 to 6 hours to the trip.

You will need to fuel your body throughout the hike. Many people fail to reach the summit because their energy stores become depleted. According to Calories Burned HQ:

A leisurely hike will burn between 300–600 calories per hour, depending on your weight, backpack, speed and terrain. The highest impacting factors for calorie burn are:

- Your weight
- The weight of any backpack you carry
- How long you're hiking for
- The distance you hike
- The speed of your hike
- The terrain you hike (cross country, uphill, downhill, etc.)
- How steep the hills are

A 150-pound person with no backpack hiking for 60 minutes at 2.5 miles per hour cross country will burn 351 calories. The same person with a 20-pound backpack on hiking for 60 minutes at a speed of 3 miles and up and down hills of 4 percent incline will burn 464 calories.

The weight of your backpack makes a big difference. Every 1 pound of backpack weight increases calorie burn by around 5 calories per 2-hour hike. Your backpack weight should not exceed 20 percent of your body weight. A 200-pound person should not exceed a backpack weight of 40 pounds. A 150-pound person should not have a backpack bigger than 30 pounds.

Based on the Mount Whitney example above, one could expect to burn 3,600 to 7,200 calories over the course of the hike.

Hydration!

In addition to your body's need for fuel, proper hydration levels must be maintained for the body to perform at its level best. A 2 percent drop in hydration levels is all that is required for the onset of acute dehydration and equates to a 10 to 12 percent decrease in the muscles' ability to do work. REI instructor Megan Stump wrote that "the adult human body is about 60 percent water, and even light exercise can deplete that percentage, leaving you feeling crummy and interfering with your athletic performance. So, whether you're hiking, biking, skiing, running, climbing or simply strolling across town, it's important to hydrate properly."

Follow these hydration tips before, during, and after a trip to the mountains, and the experience will be more enjoyable:

- Drink early and drink often. Do not wait until you feel thirsty to drink. If you are feeling thirsty, early stages of dehydration are already present. Take smaller and more frequent sips instead of gulping down water. Set an alarm as a reminder to drink and eat.

- Keep your water accessible. Use a hydration bladder with a straw or clip a water bottle to your pack so that you do not have to stop moving to take a drink.

- Prehydrate. Consume 16 to 24 ounces of water about an hour before exercise.

Nestled in the Alabama Hills below the Eastern Sierra Mountains, the Mobius Arch frames Mount Whitney, making this location a photographer's favorite. Getting there requires a short hike from the Movie Flat Road parking area.

- Rehydrate. As soon as possible after you finish the hike, start to rehydrate. This will help the body recover and be ready to go back out the next day.
- Drink more at elevation and when the temperature drops. Dehydration indicators can appear more rapidly at elevation than at sea level. As we climb higher, the desire to eat and drink may diminish, so the importance of both increases. The same things happen as the temperature drops.
- In addition to hydration levels, replenish electrolytes. The longer the duration of your activity, the more important this becomes. Sodium, potassium, manganese, and calcium are important for muscular performance. Sports drinks and electrolyte tablets are readily available for use.

Weighing in at 1 pound, 16 ounces of water will be the single heaviest item in your pack. Fortunately, throughout the fourteeners water sources are abundant. Knowing where these springs, creeks, lakes, tarns, and ponds are along your route can reduce the amount of weight being carried. It is advisable to source your water upstream from campgrounds and beaver ponds at high elevations.

When it comes to the water you drink and cook with in the backcountry, it is always a good idea to purify or filter before ingesting. The Centers for Disease Control mandates boiling water for one minute to kill any disease-bearing organisms. Aquamira, iodine tablets, or chlorine-based products can eliminate harmful pathogens in as few as five minutes. The third option is a gravity or pump filter system to remove some or all of the bacteria. There are some people who "dip and drink" right out of the source, especially when above the tree line. To avoid getting sick in the backcountry, it is strongly suggested that some precautions are taken.

There Is Danger in the Hills

Hypothermia Is Not Your Friend!

According to the Mayo Clinic:

> Hypothermia is a medical emergency that occurs when your body loses heat faster than it can produce heat, causing a dangerously low body temperature. Normal body temperature is around 98.6 F (37 C). Hypothermia (hi-poe-THUR-me-uh) occurs as your body temperature falls below 95 F (35 C). When your body temperature drops, your heart, nervous system, and other organs can't work normally. Left untreated, hypothermia can eventually lead to complete failure of your heart and respiratory system and eventually to death. Hypothermia is often caused by exposure to cold weather or immersion in cold water. Primary treatments for hypothermia are methods to warm the body back to a normal temperature.

Signs and symptoms of hypothermia include:

- Shivering
- Slurred speech or mumbling
- Slow, shallow breathing
- Weak pulse
- Clumsiness or lack of coordination
- Drowsiness or very low energy
- Confusion or memory loss
- Loss of consciousness
- Bright red, cold skin (in infants)

Altitude Sickness

Altitude sickness is a disorder caused by being at high altitude, where oxygen levels are low, without gradually getting used to the increase in altitude. It is also known as acute mountain sickness (AMS), altitude illness, hypobaropathy, Acosta disease, puna, and soroche. The condition occurs at altitudes higher than 8,000 feet (2,500 meters). Since all of the fourteeners in this book exceed 8,000 feet, altitude sickness is a very real issue. As we climb higher, the oxygen saturation level of the air we breathe decreases. Unless time is taken to acclimate to the lower oxygen levels, fluid can build up in the lungs and brain, which can lead to headaches, shortness of breath, physical weakness, and exhaustion. Altitude sickness is usually the result of climbing too high at a fast rate before the body can adjust. The primary treatment is to descend to lower elevations.

Signs and symptoms of altitude sickness include:

- Persistent headache
- Lack of appetite, nausea, or vomiting
- Exhaustion
- Dizziness
- Numbness
- Swelling of the hands, feet, and face

Thunderstorms and Lightning

Thunderstorms are common daily occurrences throughout the year in the mountains. Oftentimes they will form in the middle of the afternoon, especially in late summer. Rain increases the safety risks of hiking and climbing in the mountains. Rocks get slick when they get wet, so the chance of slipping and falling increases. The precipitation can drive a person's core temperature down and hypothermia can set in. Rain itself will not kill you. Lightning, on the other hand, can do just that. It is advisable to start descending the moment storm clouds are spotted. If you are planning a day hike, start in the early morning hours so that you can return to safety before a storm hits.

The lightning safety community reminds us that there is *no* safe place to be outside in a thunderstorm. If you absolutely can't get to safety, there are steps you can take to help lessen the threat of being struck by lightning while outside. Don't kid yourself—you are *not* safe outside. The *safest* location during lightning activity is a large enclosed building, not a picnic shelter or shed. The second-safest location is an enclosed metal vehicle (car, truck, van, etc.) but *not* a convertible, bike, or other topless or soft-top vehicle.

Being stranded outdoors when lightning is striking nearby is a harrowing experience. Your first and only truly safe choice is to get to a safe building or vehicle. If you are engaged in outdoor activities and cannot get to a safe vehicle or shelter, follow these last-resort tips. They will not prevent you from being hit, just slightly lessen the odds.

- Do *not* seek shelter under tall, isolated trees. The tree may help you stay dry but will significantly increase your risk of being struck by lightning. Rain will not kill you, but the lightning can!
- Do *not* seek shelter under partially enclosed buildings.
- Stay away from tall, isolated objects. Lightning typically strikes the tallest object. That may be you in an open field or clearing.

The campgrounds below the Whitney Portal Trailhead provide a peaceful place to acclimate for a day or two prior to your summit attempt.

- Know the weather patterns of the area. For example, in mountainous areas, thunderstorms typically develop in the early afternoon, so plan to hike early in the day and be down the mountain by noon.
- Know the weather forecast. If there is a high chance of thunderstorms, curtail your outdoor activities.
- Do not place your campsite in an open field on the top of a hill or on a ridgetop. Keep your site away from tall, isolated trees or other tall objects. If you are in a forest, stay near a lower stand of trees. If you are camping in an open area, set up camp in a valley, ravine, or other low area. A tent offers *no* protection from lighting.
- Wet ropes can make excellent conductors. This is *bad* news when it comes to lightning activity. If you are mountain climbing and see lightning, and can do so safely, remove unnecessary ropes extended or attached to you. If a rope is extended across a mountain face and lightning makes contact with it, the electrical current will likely travel along the rope, especially if it is wet.
- Stay away from metal objects, such as fences, poles, and backpacks. Metal is an excellent conductor.
- The current from a lightning flash will easily travel for long distances. If lightning is in the immediate area, and there is no safe location nearby, stay at least 15 feet apart from other members of your group so the lightning won't travel between you if hit.
- Keep your feet together and sit on the ground out in the open. If you can possibly run to a vehicle or building, *do so*. Sitting or crouching on the ground is not safe and should be a last resort if an enclosed building or vehicle is not available.

Wind

Downslope winds occur when warm/dry air descends rapidly down a mountainside. In the Sierras, winds can gust in excess of 60 miles per hour and can make staying upright on the trail challenging. For summits with exposure, even a 10 mph wind can be dangerous. Knowing the forecast before leaving the trailhead can help ensure that you return safe and sound.

Bears!

Seeing animals in the wild can be a breathtaking experience. Bighorn sheep, mule deer, and marmots can commonly be seen during your hike. While sightings are not as common, black bears inhabit the entire Sierra Nevada mountain range. Bears are usually sighted between the valley floors and the tree line at 10,500 feet. While black bears do not usually pose a threat to humans, many have become habituated to having people around and are skilled at taking unattended food.

In the Sierras both the NFS and NPS require all food to be stored in bear-proof containers. These can be either a hard-shell canister or a scent-proof bag.

Bags should be hung 15 feet in the air and a minimum of 30 feet from camp. To help preserve the flora, is it preferred that either a dead tree or a rock is utilized in hanging a food cache. Since the ideal hanging scenario can be difficult to find, a food canister is the smarter way to protect your food. Canisters can be rented when you pick up your permit or purchased prior to arrival. Many of the trailheads and campgrounds have metal bear-proof lockers. Place any food or scented items in these before departing up the trail. Bears can recognize food items left in a car and are adept at breaking in.

Encountering a bear at a distance can be amazing to watch. However, occasionally, you may come face-to-face with a bear, changing the experience dramatically. The experts at Bearsmart.com offer this advice:

If you encounter a bear on the trail, or in your campsite, stop what you are doing and evaluate the situation. Identify yourself by speaking in a calm, appeasing tone. Back away slowly, preferably in the direction you came. Walk, don't run, and keep your eye on the bear so you can see how it will react. In most cases, the bear will flee.

If you are in your campsite or other place bears shouldn't be, and you are sure the bear is a black bear, consider trying to move it out of the area. Ensure the bear has a clear and safe escape route with no people or obstacles in its way. Stand tall and look it directly in the eye. Yell at the bear and firmly tell it to leave: "Get out of here, bear!" Keep a can of pepper spray ready (with the safety removed) in case the bear approaches too closely. . . .

Occasionally, a bear will approach you in a nondefensive manner. It may just be curious. Perhaps it's a young adult bear that is simply testing its dominance. Or it is food conditioned and/or habituated. Very rarely, it may see you as potential prey.

In any event, talk to the bear in a firm voice. Get out of its way if you can, which may be all it wants. If the bear follows you and its attention is clearly directed at you, then stand your ground and prepare to use your deterrent. A bear that is initially curious or testing you may become predatory if you do not stand up to it.

Act aggressively. Look it straight in the eyes and let it know you will fight if attacked. Shout! Make yourself look as big as possible. Stamp your feet and take a step or two toward the bear. Threaten the bear with whatever is handy (stick, pole, bear spray). The more the bear persists, the more aggressive your response should be.

If the bear attacks, use your deterrent and fight for your life. Kick, punch or hit the bear with whatever weapon is available. Concentrate your attack on the face, eyes, and nose. Fight any bear that attacks you in your building or tent.

Any trip into the backcountry starts long before you reach the trail. The kit you take with you can keep you warm, dry, and fed all the way to the summit—or, with a lack of planning, can leave you miserable at the side of the trail. If you get caught in a backcountry emergency situation without the right equipment, the consequences could be catastrophic. Each item you will need should be purchased well in advance of your trip. Wear it. Touch it. Set it up in the yard several times. Be familiar with each piece *before* you start to climb. Having a comfort level with your equipment will prepare you for the unique situations waiting on the mountain.

Depending on your budget, each item needed for a positive experience can be purchased at a big-box sporting goods store or at a specialty outfitter. Items purchased at big-box chain stores, such as Scheels or Dick's, may save in initial cost but will likely add weight and bulk to your pack over a kit purchased at an outdoor specialty store. The actual outdoor experience of the salesperson may also be lacking in this type of retail environment. The specialty outfitter will provide a level of service, expertise, and knowledge when it comes to equipment choices. You will find a myriad of choices in lightweight and high-quality gear in a specialty store.

Outfitters like Big Willi Mountaineering in Lone Pine (at the base of Mount Whitney) are owned by people who live and play in the Sierras. Recreational Equipment Inc. (REI) is a major outdoor specialty chain with stores across the country. Consulting with the experienced staff in stores that focus on the outdoors will be a huge asset—they have been there and done that. Chances are they have made mistakes, and learned from them, over the years. The knowledge and education that can be gleaned from those with experience can prove vital in choosing where you spend your money and what gear to buy.

Whether you will be camping at the trailhead and climbing to the summit and back in a day or are planning for several days in the backcountry will dictate what you need to carry on your back and what you can leave in the car. The following pieces of gear should be with you no matter the duration of your expedition.

Let's Talk Shoes

Wear your boots or shoes not just while training for your adventure, but while running errands around town. This will allow you to get used to the weight and stability of a shoe designed to protect your feet from the rocks and trail you will encounter on the way to the summit. More importantly, you will be able to identify any areas where your foot and the shoe rub, slip, or slide. Many trips have the fun sapped right out of them by painful blisters. Pair your choice of footwear with a quality sock. If your feet go bad during a hike, you will not enjoy the result.

With so many footwear choices on the market, the decision between a traditional hiking boot and a sturdy trail running shoe comes down to personal preference. The trail and footing will change dramatically once the tree line has been reached at approximately 10,000 feet.

Traditional boots provide solid ankle support and rock protection along with a stable platform. Compared to a trail shoe, a boot will weigh almost twice as much. However, weight savings mean a loss in the protection and stability department. Boots are recommended for multiday hikes, for trips (like Mount Shasta) that will take you above the snow line, and for especially rocky approaches like the 99 switchbacks on the way to Mount Whitney. Experienced hikers may be able to utilize a trail shoe with a rock plate on light and fast ascents.

From most trailheads to the tree line, the hiking surface will be dirt-based. There will be some rocks and roots, but mostly hard-packed dirt will be underfoot. Once you pass the tree line, the trail will increasingly become more and more rocky. Cumbersome talus, slippery scree, and tennis-ball-size granite rocks will greet your feet as you approach the summits. Many of the approaches involve crossing streams or creeks. Keeping your shoes, socks, and feet dry are vital to a successful and enjoyable summit. Wet shoes, socks, and feet are a good combination for issues such as hot spots, chafing, and blisters. Always pack extra dry socks just in case you cannot avoid a water crossing.

Putting one step in front of the other is the only way to reach the summit. Keeping your feet protected, blister-free, and dry comes down to your choice of footwear and socks. The debate over hiking boots versus trail running shoes will continue on. Hiking boots provide a level of protection against the granite the Sierras are formed from. Not only will boots provide ankle support, but they will also prevent the rocks you step on from poking through the soles and into your feet. The drawback is that boots can be heavy and hot compared to trail shoes. You will definitely want to wear your boots around the house and out and about before you reach the trail. A trail running shoe will provide more protection than a regular running shoe. Wearing a lightweight and breathable trail shoe means you will use less energy each step you take compared to a boot. However, while many trail shoes have built-in rock plates, you lose the support and protection a boot provides. Only you can decide where the tradeoff line is when it comes to the type of footwear you choose.

One good rule no matter what type of footwear you choose for your climb is to buy a half size larger than you normally would. Over several hours, or several days, of hiking your feet are going to swell. Over time gravity draws fluid to the lower extremities. This edema can swell your feet a half to a full size larger than normal. To accommodate for potential swelling, a slightly larger size shoe is recommended.

Socks are very personal to each of us. With that in mind, stay away from cotton socks when you're on the trail. Choose a wool or synthetic fabric sock depending on the time of year. Wool retains the ability to keep you warm even when it gets wet. Synthetic materials wick the moisture away from your feet. Keeping your feet dry will diminish the potential for blisters and hot spots. On the trail, you will want to keep your feet as dry as possible and avoid travel through water.

Preparing for the Palisades, Nick Niforos uses the Alabama Hills between Lone Pine and Mount Whitney as a secluded place to organize his Leki poles and Petzl gear. Make sure to inspect your harness and rope for wear spots before reaching the trailhead.

Carrying and Packing Your Gear

A backpack will carry everything you need into the backcountry. A pack with one main compartment will save some weight, while one with pockets and compartments will allow for better organization and make getting to your gear easier. There are internal- and external-framed packs that have a defined shape and structure to provide both support and comfort. You will also find frameless packs that weigh less than their cousins with frames. Choose a pack that fits your body and your needs. Pack-fitting is an area in which the outdoor specialty/outfitter shop excels over a big-box store. Ideally, you would have multiple packs for a variety of activities, as a day hike requires far less space requirements than does a multiday expedition.

Companies such as Osprey make a wide variety of packs to fit any hiker's needs. The way a pack fits on your back and body will also be vital to a trip's comfort level. Look for a fit that allows air flow between your back and the pack itself. This space will keep your back cool and minimize potential hot spots created when the pack rubs against your body. A good pack will feature shoulder and chest straps along with a padded waist belt that can be adjusted while you are moving up the trail.

Some packs come equipped with a separate hydration compartment. Since one of the challenges of hiking at elevation will be to maintain hydration levels, a bladder with a drinking straw will be a constant reminder to drink. The human body is composed mostly of water. A 2 percent decrease in your body's hydration level equates to a 15 percent decrease in the muscles' ability to do work.

A pack such as the Osprey Volt, which met all of my needs during the research for this book, will also have internal compartments and pockets to help organize your gear. With external tie-downs, daisy chains, equipment loops, and pockets, you should be able to pack and secure your gear so that it doesn't wag like a tail behind you. Since for every action there is an equal and opposite reaction, flopping gear off the back of your pack will cause your core area to move in the opposite direction to maintain balance. The ultimate goal is to move up the trail in an efficient forward motion.

This style pack works great for multiday hikes where you will encounter varying weather and trail conditions requiring specific clothing and gear. For many, each hike to a fourteener summit will be over two or three days. A tent, sleeping bag, camp stove, jacket and extra clothing, food, water, and the rest of your gear should be able to fit in a 60-liter pack. Depending on how long you're planning on being in the backcountry and what equipment fills your pack, you might have between 20 and 40 pounds on your back.

For many of the mountains in this book, hiking a portion of the trail on the first day would be advisable. This allows for your body to acclimate and recover fully for the summit push. Camping below the summit will also let you remove some weight from your pack. Leaving your tent and sleeping bag at the campsite eliminates both bulk and pounds from your pack as well as leaving you a comfortable place to recover after reaching the top.

Very fit and strong hikers may want to push from the trailhead to the summit in one day. This mindset changes not only what pack will be carried, but what gear goes inside as well. Attacking Mount Whitney up the main trail can take up to a full 24 hours for most people. Since these individuals will likely not pack a tent or sleeping bag, a smaller-volume pack should be sufficient. The same pack can be used for second-day summit approaches. The Mons Peak IX 30-liter roll-top pack is the ideal size for a one-day attack on the summit.

What Do I Wear?

There is a Norwegian saying that goes, "There is no such thing as bad weather, only bad clothing." An enjoyable trip to the backcountry should embrace this saying. The clothing choices made before reaching the trail can have a profound effect on the success of your hike. The layers you wear will protect your skin from the sun, rocks, plants, and changing weather conditions. In the mountains, select base layers made from wool or synthetic fabrics over cotton. These materials will wick moisture away from the skin, will dry quickly, and will help maintain your body's core temperature. In general, for every 1,000 feet of elevation gain, the ambient temperature will drop 7 degrees Fahrenheit (4 degrees Celsius). If the trailhead has an elevation of 6,000 feet and the summit reaches 14,000 feet, the temperature difference between the two points will be more than 50 degrees F (28 degrees C). As you climb higher, the ultraviolet intensity increases 8 to 10 percent per 1,000 feet of elevation gain.

Choose breathable tops and bottoms that can be layered as the changing trail conditions warrant. Plan to dress for the conditions on the summit so that you can enjoy and appreciate the work it took to get there. At the trailhead you might be wearing shorts and short sleeves, while at the summit that could change to a jacket, gloves, and long pants. Make sure there is a waterproof, windproof jacket, such as the Outdoor Research Interstellar jacket, in your pack, as weather conditions can change rapidly in the mountains. Over a six-day period while researching this book, I encountered thunderstorms with lightning, gale-force winds, snow, triple-digit temperatures, and a wildfire. Be prepared for all potential weather conditions. I am a big fan of the Outdoor Research Ferrosi hiking pants and shorts for their durability and lightweight breathable properties and used them exclusively during my climbing trips.

Temperatures can change drastically in the mountains, and you need to consider what, if any, outerwear will go into your kit. In addition to the rain jacket, it may be advisable to include something a bit warmer just in case. In case of what? In case you get caught in an unexpected snowstorm. In case your day turns into night. In case you reach the summit of Mount Whitney to find 20 mph winds, making it feel less than freezing. In case you do not want to become hypothermic. In 2019, several people had to be rescued from the mountains in varying degrees of hypothermia. Having an outer layer in your pack can actually be a lifesaver. The Himali Annapurna Softshell jacket offers warmth in addition to being waterproof and windproof and

One of two of the California fourteeners not in the eastern Sierras, the summit of White Mountain offers views of the Sierras to the west, the Owens Valley below, and Nevada to the east. The entire trail sits above the tree line and offers little protection from the elements.

was the ideal jacket to summit Mount Shasta in. The Terracea Station parka provided full-length coverage while hiking through the snow up and over Shepards Pass.

Shelter and Warmth

If camping is in the plan, a tent and sleeping bag will be in order. These two items, along with a sleeping pad, will provide a sheltered place to recover from the day's hiking.

Depending on the time of year, the specific mountain, and how many will be in your party, the type of tent you take will vary. During the traditional climbing season (April–October) in the Sierras, a three-season tent will provide sufficient shelter, as extreme cold and snow is usually not an issue. The tent will be one of the heaviest pieces of equipment in your pack, but without the shelter it provides, you will be at the mercy of Mother Nature. We used the ultralight Big Agnes Copper Spur Platinum and the Mons Peak IX Trail 21 tents while climbing and researching over 18 months for this book. From freak snowstorms to gale-force winds to perfect bluebird days, we were dry and warm.

Having solid shelter is part of the rest and recovery equation, as you are protected from the elements. By choosing the incorrect sleeping bag for the expected conditions, you could end up shivering or sweating instead of sleeping. Always check the forecast while packing for your trip. If the projected low temperature is going to be 50 degrees F (10 degrees C), taking a sleeping bag rated for 0 degrees F/-18 degrees C will be too hot. Conversely, using a bag rated at 50 degrees F/10 degrees C will be inefficient at keeping you warm when the temperature dips into the teens.

Our Western Mountaineering Kodiak (0 degrees F) and Highlite (35 degrees F), Mons Peak IX Settler (15 degrees F), and Big Agnes Beryl ((0 degrees F) and Pluton (40 degrees F) covered a wide range of temperatures and conditions.

Other Equipment

Whether you are planning to hike over one or several days, there are some items that you should not head up the trail without.

First-aid kit: Including bandages, gauze pads, medical tape, blister pads/second skin, antibacterial ointment, and an elastic wrap. You can purchase a preassembled kit or can make your own.

Headlamp: Chances are at some point during a hike, you will encounter low-light conditions. A headlamp provides a beam of light to guide you down the trail while keeping your hands free.

Map and compass: Even though we are becoming more and more reliant on battery-powered devices for navigation, knowing how to use a traditional map and compass will help keep you on the correct route whether you have phone service or not.

Sunscreen: As noted above, the intensity of the sun's rays increases as you climb higher. Protecting exposed skin from burning will make your trip more enjoyable.

During late spring and early summer hikes you may encounter rapid flowing stream crossings. Some-times there may be dead fall and brush making for challenging footing. CHRISTIE CHRISTIANSON

Bug spray: Blackflies and mosquitoes can be found from the spring into late fall, making camping and stopping along the trail a buzzkill.

Global Positioning System (GPS) tracking device: The Bivystick provides each user with a unique URL that can be shared with friends and family so they can follow the user's progress from home. The user can send and receive text messages, check weather reports, and access maps as well as send SOS distress signals in case of emergency.

Trekking poles: If two legs are good, four legs are better. Trekking poles help provide stability on slick and loose trails, aid in traction, and disperse weight while hiking. Mons Peak IX offers three different poles to fit any budget.

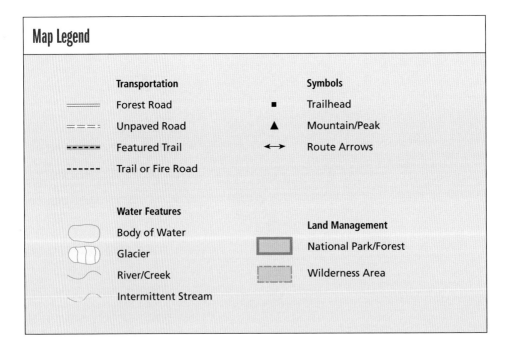

Map Legend

Transportation		Symbols	
═══════	Forest Road	▪	Trailhead
═ ═ ═ ═	Unpaved Road	▲	Mountain/Peak
▪▪▪▪▪▪	Featured Trail	←→	Route Arrows
▪ ▪ ▪ ▪ ▪	Trail or Fire Road		

Water Features		Land Management	
	Body of Water		National Park/Forest
	Glacier		Wilderness Area
	River/Creek		
	Intermittent Stream		

1 Mount Langley

Elevation: 14,025 feet, 11th highest
Start: Cottonwood Lakes
Distance: 18 miles round-trip
Primary route: Old Army Pass Trail to Southwest Slope
Elevation gain: 4,025 feet
Hiking time: 7 to 10 hours
Difficulty: Class 1, Class 2
Trail surface: Dirt trail leading to scree
Trailhead elevation: 10,000 feet
Camping: Paid campsites at trailhead, dispersed camping along trail

Fees: None
Permit: Yes
Best seasons: Summer and fall
Maps: Tom Harrison Mt. Whitney Zone, Mt. Whitney High Country
Nearest town: Lone Pine, CA
Trail contact: Mount Whitney Ranger District, PO Box 8, Lone Pine, CA 93545; (760) 876-6200
First ascent: 1864, William Bellows

Finding the trailhead: From Lone Pine, at the intersection of US 395 and Whitney Portal Road, head west (toward the mountains). At 3.2 miles, turn left (south) on Horseshoe Meadow Road. At 22.5 miles, turn right (north), following the sign to New Army Pass and Cottonwood Lakes. At 23 miles, arrive at the Cottonwood Lakes Trailhead. Park in a designated space and walk past the interpretive display to reach the trail. GPS: 36.52330°N / 118.238°W

The Hike

At 14,025 feet, Mount Langley may be one of the shortest mountains in the group, but do not show up unprepared for this one. Langley is the southernmost of the fourteeners and is very accessible throughout most of the year. Along with White Mountain, we like to use Mount Langley as a starter fourteener. The hike up is not as technical as many of the others, but the final 1,000 feet will steal your breath and get your attention. You can summit Mount Langley during all seasons, but the best times are from May to early October. You can reserve your permit in advance using Recreation.gov, or you can try to obtain a permit by walking in to the visitor center. To ensure you get a permit, apply well in advance of your trip.

Credit for the first ascent of Langley goes to either William Bellows in 1864 or geologist Clarence King and Frenchman Paul Pinson on June 22, 1871, believing they were actually on Mount Whitney, which lies 6 miles to the north. According to the *Inyo Independent*, on July 19, 1872, a party that included the first woman (the wife of the Inyo County Sheriff) reached the peak. This third party reported finding three separate summit cairns. King, in his book *Mountaineering in the Sierra Nevada*, wrote that upon reaching the summit, a "mound of rock was piled upon the peak, and solidly built into an arrow shaft pointing due west." Bellows was reported to have built one in 1864 (*Inyo Independent*). The creator of the third cairn reported by Sheriff Mulkey remains unknown.

Mount Langley comes into view as you reach the Cottonwood Lakes just a few miles up the trail. If you leave the trailhead early enough, the soft glow of the sun will bathe your destination in orange. Later in the day, you will see the stark gray of the granite face.

From Hidden Lake, Mount Langley's summit looks inviting. You still have a few thousand feet of elevation to cover before you can view the lake from above.

After picking up your permit at the Eastern Sierra Interagency Visitor Center (at the intersection of CA 136 and US 395), head west out of Lone Pine on Whitney Portal Road, passing the Alabama Hills on your right. Turning left on Horseshoe Meadow Road takes you right to the Cottonwood Lakes Trailhead. Make sure that Horseshoe Meadow Road is open to vehicle traffic, or you will be in for a 12- to 14-mile hike to the trailhead. Expect the road to be closed from November through mid-April depending on the snowpack. During the winter you can snowshoe or cross-country ski into the trailhead. There is a large interpretive display marking the start of the trail.

The 18-mile hike to the summit and back can be done in a day, or you can camp halfway up the trail at Cottonwood Lakes. This hike has a gradual elevation gain of only about 4,000 feet. Leaving the parking area, it will take you almost 3 miles to gain 1,000 feet of elevation, making for a pleasant and nontechnical hike. The most popular, and the safest and easiest, route will be taking the Cottonwood Lakes Trail to the Old Army Pass Trail. You will find good footing and water sources along the trail. Depending on the time of year you are hiking, the meadows may be lush with wildflowers. Mount Langley will first come into view as the trail passes Cottonwood Lake #1. In the early morning light, the tallest peak to the north takes on an orange glow. Later in the day, the starkness of the granite becomes dominant.

Dispersed camping near the Cottonwood Lakes brings a peace and serenity that can only be found hidden in the backcountry. Bear canisters or bags are mandatory for food items. Make sure to place or hang them at least 30 feet away from your tent. Campfires are not allowed in this area, and you should always purify drinking and cooking water. It is advisable to pack a waterproof jacket, as there is potential for afternoon storms throughout the year.

Once you get above the tree line at around 10,500 feet, the potential for exposure to the sun increases. While the ambient temperature will drop about 10 degrees for every 1,000 feet higher you go, the intensity of the sun increases. Likely you will not feel hot, but the time it takes for the sun to burn your skin diminishes. Wear a wide-brimmed hat, like the Sombroilet from Outdoor Research, to protect your face, ears, and neck from the sun. Long sleeves and pants made from synthetic materials provide an additional layer of protection from the sun. The trail is a nice, worn dirt path from the trailhead to Cottonwood Lakes. Once you start up the switchbacks, the dirt gives way to granite.

Continue on the Old Army Pass Trail around Cottonwood Lake #5, and you will find the steepest part of the hike. The trail snakes its way up a granite cliff, gaining more than 1,000 feet in just over a half mile. You may encounter some snow and/or ice on this section, as the cliff shades the trail from the sun. Depending on the conditions, it may be necessary to use crampons or micro-spikes to provide traction. Look closely and you just may see bighorn sheep watching your progress.

Once you gain the pass, the views in all directions are stunning. The hike from here to the summit follows a trail to the north. The trail will veer slightly west at times. Do not be tempted to travel cross-country to the base of Langley on a direct north/northeast bearing. Taking this route will turn your day into a Class 4 experience with lots of exposed free scrambling. The preferred route will bring you to the base of Mount Langley slightly west of the actual summit.

Once you reach the final approach, look for the giant, Volkswagen-size cairns. The National Forest Service has constructed these stacked rock formations to help hikers follow the easiest and safest path to the summit. The final 1,000 feet of elevation to the summit climbs over scree and talus. It is easy to wander off-trail in the final section, and if you happen to do just that, keep making upward progress until you gain the plateau just below the summit. The loose scree will make it seem like you're taking one step up and sliding a half step down.

The summit marker and climber's register box will be located on the highest point. When you take your summit pictures, be mindful of the steep drop-offs to the north and west. The easiest way back to the trailhead will be to retrace your steps down the trail.

Extended Route: Whitney Portal Trail to Horseshoe Meadow

Finding the trailhead: From Lone Pine, at the intersection of US 395 and Whitney Portal Road, head west (toward the mountains). In 13 miles, arrive at the Whitney Portal Trailhead parking area. GPS: 36.57860°N / 118.293°W

This multiday route starts at the Whitney Portal Trailhead and will require an overnight permit. Since this hike finishes at the Cottonwood Lakes Trailhead at Horseshoe Meadow, you will either need to arrange for shuttle service or other transportation or hike back to your vehicle. This route passes near the approaches to both Mount Muir and Mount Whitney, so the ability to summit three fourteeners in one trip is very possible.

Begin hiking up the trail just steps from the Whitney Portal Store. Depending on the season and time of day, expect to encounter up to 100 people a day on the way to Trail Crest. There are two designated camping locations along the eastern approach. Outpost Camp and Trail Camp are the only locations where pitching a tent is allowed on the way up the trail.

Reaching these locations will take several hours for most people, and the luxury of stretching out and relaxing before the final summit push will be welcome. Situated above the tree line, Trail Camp does not offer much in the way of protection from the sun, so choose your spot wisely. The camp lies just below the start of Whitney's infamous 99 switchbacks, so you can get a look at the 2 miles of granite trail waiting for you.

For a variety of reasons, it is smart to get an early start on your summit push. Once you start the next section of the hike, there will not be any consistent protection from the sun that beats down on the trail. Leaving at a predawn hour will eliminate most of the blazing sun on the way up. Since the trail traffic is regulated by permits, starting early will also help avoid getting caught behind slower groups on the trail.

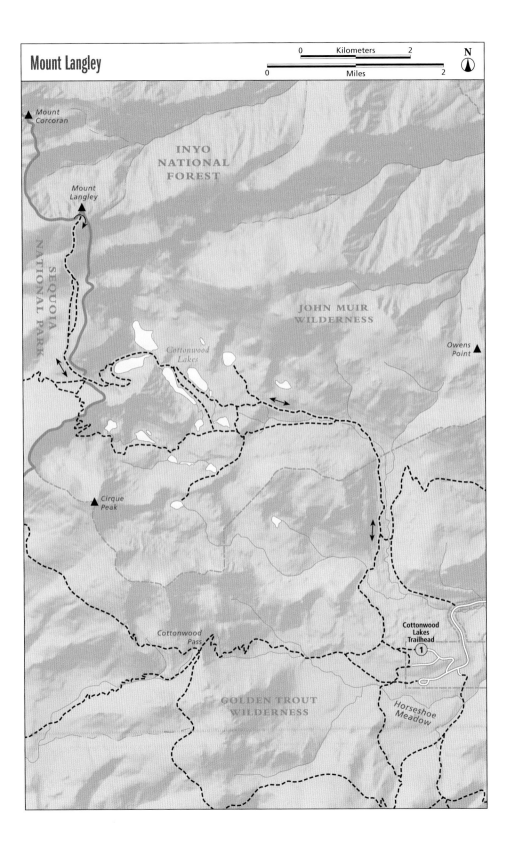

Mount Langley

Kilometers 0 — 2

Miles 0 — 2

N

Mount Corcoran

INYO
NATIONAL
FOREST

Mount Langley

SEQUOIA NATIONAL PARK

JOHN MUIR
WILDERNESS

Cottonwood
Lakes

Owens Point

Cirque Peak

Cottonwood Lakes Trailhead
1

Cottonwood Pass

GOLDEN TROUT
WILDERNESS

Horseshoe Meadow

Thunderstorms can arrive without much advance warning in the afternoon. Getting caught on an exposed ridge in a lightning storm will potentially result in serious injury, so plan to be down before afternoon.

Mentally, there is an advantage to leaving in the dark. The actual hiking distance from Trail Camp to Trail Crest on the switchbacks is 2.2 miles. The direct distance is about half of that, which means that in roughly 1 mile the elevation changes 1,140 feet. The switchbacks meander up the cliff face at a pitch that most can hike with relative ease. Traversing back and forth every few minutes, the pass at Trail Crest pops in and out of view. It becomes easy to look too far ahead and feel like the progress being made is not much progress at all. Leaving Trail Camp while it is still dark eliminates the ability to look too far up the trail. You can only focus on the trail that your headlamp illuminates right in front of you. Looking up, Trail Crest will not be visible. Looking down will reveal the headlamps of other climbers on the trail behind you. This section can be a bottleneck, as the travel pace will be relatively slow.

In the spring, early summer, and late fall, you may encounter snow and ice covering the trail above the tree line. Travel from Trail Camp to Trail Crest will not utilize the famous switchbacks; rather, you will use your crampons and ice axe to traverse

Cottonwood Lake #5 will be one of the many water sources to choose from between the trailhead and the top of Old Army Pass. Purifying, or filtering, any water you are planning to drink or cook with is advisable in this area.

the chute. An understanding of how these pieces of equipment should be used is necessary before showing up at the trailhead. Make sure your ice axe has a leash so that it does not slide away from you if it falls. Always keep your axe in your uphill hand. Practice self-arrest techniques with the ice axe so that you can react quickly should you start to slide down the mountain. Your ice axe can save you from injury or worse. Crampons provide an additional level of traction while walking on frozen surfaces. Please seek instruction from a trained professional on how to use these ice tools.

If you do not possess the skills to competently use an ice axe and crampons, *do not* attempt to climb the chute to Trail Crest. You should call ahead for current weather conditions to be prepared. Due to the lottery system for Mount Whitney permits, many people approach the mountain without taking the trail conditions into consideration, feeling that since they "won" a permit, they have to attempt the climb. Summit fever can be a dangerous thing. While dehydration and altitude sickness commonly occur when the trail is clear, the consequences are far greater when snow and ice are present.

Once Trail Crest has been gained, look for the intersection of the John Muir Trail (JMT) coming up from the valley floor to the west. It will only take a few moments of hiking to find the trail. It is important to note that the approaches to both Mount Muir and Mount Whitney are within 2 miles of the junction.

2 Mount Muir

Elevation: 14,012 feet, 14th highest
Start: Whitney Portal Trailhead
Distance: 18 miles round-trip
Primary route: Mount Whitney Trail to West Face
Elevation gain: 7,867 feet
Hiking time: 14 to 20 hours
Difficulty: Class 1, Class 2/3
Trail surface: Dirt trail leading to scree, low-exposure scramble
Trailhead elevation: 8,360 feet
Camping: Designated campsites near trailhead, dispersed camping at Outpost Camp and Trail Camp

Fees: None
Permit: Yes
Best seasons: Summer and fall; technical winter climb
Maps: Tom Harrison Mt. Whitney Zone, Mt. Whitney High Country; National Geographic #322: Mt. Whitney; Wilderness Press Mt. Whitney; USGS Mount Whitney
Nearest town: Lone Pine, CA
Trail contact: Mount Whitney Ranger District, PO Box 8, Lone Pine, CA 93545; (760) 876-6200
First ascent: 1919, LeRoy Jeffers

Finding the trailhead: From Lone Pine, at the intersection of US 395 and Whitney Portal Road, head west (toward the mountains). In 13 miles, arrive at the Whitney Portal Trailhead parking area. GPS: 36.57860°N / 118.293°W

The Hike

Most Popular Route: Whitney Portal Trail

Arriving at Whitney Portal with the right equipment and fitness level puts you ahead of the summit game. Knowing how your gear fits and works and where it is in your pack before setting out will increase your success level. Put in some training time prior to showing up at the trail. Constantly trekking uphill as the oxygen content of the air you are breathing diminishes will definitely stress your body.

Drink early and drink often. Staying hydrated is a vital part of your successful summit. In addition to starting out with bottles and hydration bladders full at the trailhead, several water sources can be found along the way up the mountain. You will cross the first creek within a few minutes on the trail. Just below the start of the 99 switchbacks, at Trail Camp, you will find the last consistent water source before the summit. As with all mountain streams, ponds, and lakes, it is wise to filter or purify all water used for drinking or cooking to protect yourself from bacteria.

The temperature and weather conditions can, and will, change dramatically as you make your way toward 14,012 feet. For every 1,000 feet in elevation you gain, 10 degrees in ambient temperature will be lost. An air temperature of 60 degrees F (15 degrees C) at the trailhead will become 40 degrees F (4 degrees C) at Outpost Camp and 20 degrees F (−6 degrees C) at Trail Camp. It will be even colder, and windy, at

Mount Whitney looms above the drive into Whitney Portal, inviting you to climb to her top and enjoy the view from the tallest point in the lower 48 states. The effort and strength required to reach the summit will make signing the registry worth it.

the summit. Having the right gear and layers will protect you from the elements all the way to the summit and back.

The most popular way to reach the summit successfully includes camping along the trail. Depending on the length of your permit, you will be assigned a campsite at one of two locations. Camp only in designated areas, and make sure to hang your food bag or canister at least 30 feet from your tent. At an elevation of 10,360 feet, Outpost Camp lies just over 3 miles from the trailhead. The trail to get to the camp is easy to follow, and overnighting here will allow your body to acclimate slightly to the change in elevation. You will still find shade and cover from the forest at this elevation. For many people, this is a perfect day one stopping point.

Three more miles (and approximately another 2,000 feet) up lies Trail Camp. Those looking for a two-day summit attempt will choose to bivy at this higher camp at the end of the first day. Reaching this location will take several hours for most people, and the luxury of stretching out and relaxing before the final summit push will be welcome. Situated above the tree line, Trail Camp does not offer much in the way of protection from the sun, so choose your spot wisely. The camp lies just below the start of Whitney's infamous 99 switchbacks, so you can get a look at the 2 miles of granite trail waiting for you.

For a variety of reasons, it is smart to get an early start on your summit push. Once you start the next section of the hike, there will not be any consistent protection from the sun that beats down on the trail. Leaving at a predawn hour will eliminate most of the blazing sun on the way up. Since the trail traffic is regulated by permits, starting early will help avoid getting caught behind slower groups on the trail. Thunderstorms can arrive without much advance warning in the afternoon. Getting caught on an exposed ridge in a lightning storm will potentially result in serious injury, so plan to be down before afternoon.

Mentally, there is an advantage to leaving in the dark. The actual hiking distance from Trail Camp to Trail Crest on the switchbacks is 2.2 miles. The direct distance is about half of that, which means that in roughly 1 mile the elevation changes 1,140 feet. The switchbacks meander up the cliff face at a pitch that most can hike with relative ease. Traversing back and forth every few minutes, the pass at Trail Crest pops in and out of view. It becomes easy to look too far ahead and feel like the progress being made is not much progress at all. Leaving Trail Camp while it is still dark eliminates the ability to look too far up the trail. You can only focus on the trail that your headlamp illuminates right in front of you. Looking up, Trail Crest will not be visible. Looking down will reveal the headlamps of other climbers on the trail behind you. This section can be a bottleneck, as the travel pace will be relatively slow.

In the spring, early summer, and late fall, you may encounter snow and ice covering the trail above the tree line. Travel from Trail Camp to Trail Crest will not utilize the famous switchbacks; rather, you will use your crampons and ice axe to traverse the chute. An understanding of how these pieces of equipment should be used is necessary before showing up at the trailhead. Make sure your ice axe has a leash so that it does not slide away from you if it falls. Always keep your axe in your uphill hand. Practice self-arrest techniques with the ice axe so that you can react quickly should you start to slide down the mountain. Your ice axe can save you from injury or worse. Crampons provide an additional level of traction while walking on frozen surfaces. Please seek instruction from a trained professional on how to use these ice tools.

If you do not possess the skills to competently use an ice axe and crampons, *do not* attempt to climb the chute to Trail Crest. You should call ahead for current weather conditions to be prepared. Due to the lottery system for Mount Whitney permits, many people approach the mountain without taking the trail conditions into consideration, feeling that since they "won" a permit, they have to attempt the climb. Summit fever can be a dangerous thing. While dehydration and altitude sickness commonly occur when the trail is clear, the consequences are far greater when snow and ice are present.

Without adequate training and skills with both crampons and ice axe, you will endanger not only yourself but those around you as well. The physical exertion of climbing combined with the unpredictable footing that ice and snow provide can lead to slips and falls. Falls of this nature can go for hundreds of feet, resulting in injury, rescue, and, in extreme cases, death. Be mindful of your party's skill set if you

Some of the most captivating views from Trail Crest to the summit of Whitney will be to the west. The reflection of Hitchcock Mountain in the Hitchcock Lakes below is just one example. From this point you will also be able to see the John Muir Trail snaking its way up the mountain to join you.

encounter frozen conditions. The mountain will always be there, and you can always try again if the danger level seems high.

Once you reach Trail Crest, there will be just 1 more mile and less than 900 feet in elevation to climb. This last section provides the most exposure as you traverse the ridgeline. There are some very steep drop-offs on both sides of the trail, so be mindful of where your feet go. The John Muir Trail (JMT) climbs up from the west and intersects with the Whitney approach about a half mile past Trail Crest.

a well-defined and -maintained trail. The trail crosses to the north side of the creek and leads you to a granite cliff face. At this point expect the trail to be difficult to follow at times.

Maintain the north side of the creek for just over a quarter mile of distance. Your waypoint will be the large "Matterhorn" rock formation. Once you reach the way-point, scramble your way onto the Ebersbacher Ledges above you. Continue to work through the steep ledges east and then west as you gain elevation. Take your time and watch where you place your feet. Once you have reached the top ledge, hike around the base of the granite cliff until Lower Boy Scout Lake is reached. While only a short distance into the hike, campsites can be found here.

From Lower Boy Scout Lake to Upper Boy Scout Lake, maintaining your route can become challenging. You will encounter several trail options. Take the trail found just above the willow trees. You may encounter route cairns that will help guide you through the talus and rocky slabs that lie between the two lakes. The distance from the trailhead to Upper Boy Scout Lake will be just a shade over 3.5 miles. Avoid bushwhacking through the willow trees and undergrowth. If you are planning on making this a multiday trip, set up camp here. This location also makes a great approach point to Mount Russell.

Leaving Upper Boy Scout Lake with 2.5 miles remaining to the summit of Mount Whitney, the trail crosses through a glacial moraine. Once you reach the top of the moraine, the trail heads toward the creek. Depending on the time of year, you may pass a waterfall and find water seeping from the cliffside. Continue west until you encounter a break in the cliff that will allow you to scramble up through scree and some ledges. Since there may be some water crossings in this steep section, be mindful that your feet may slip on the rocks due to wet shoes.

Work your way up the trail until you reach Iceberg Lake. Mount Whitney will be directly above you. The Mountaineer's Route follows the large gully visible to the right (north) of Mount Whitney. Depending on the time of year and the winter snowpack, you may need to use crampons and an ice axe to make your way up this couloir. If snow can be avoided, there is an abundance of solid hand- and footholds for use. At just over 14,000 feet you reach the notch at the top of the couloir. Mount Russell's east ridge approach can be made from this point.

From the notch, drop down to the water-stained gully to your left. Once in the gully, ascend using the ledges on both sides to climb the final few hundred feet to the summit of Mount Whitney. Continue down the Whitney Portal Trail for just over a mile until you encounter the Mount Muir summit approach.

Often hikers will leave their backpacks on the side of the trail while they ascend the Class 3 scramble to the summit block. You may have to lean into the rock faces and use your hands to balance and traverse the route to the summit. Expect the final 600-vertical-foot climb to have a little exposure and take up to an hour to complete. As you begin the ascent from the John Muir Trail, expect to find some loose material. While not really scree, your footing may feel a bit unstable.

Mount Muir and Mount Whitney: Mountaineer's Route

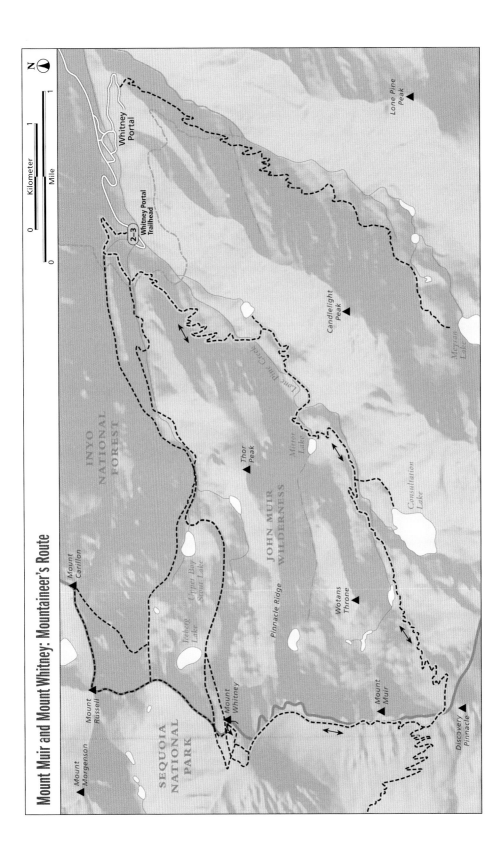

N

Kilometer
0   1

Mile
0   1

Whitney Portal

Whitney Portal Trailhead

2–3

Mount Carillon

INYO NATIONAL FOREST

Lone Pine Creek

Candlelight Peak

Meysan Lake

Mount Morgenson

Mount Russell

Iceberg Lake

Upper Boy Scout Lake

Thor Peak

JOHN MUIR WILDERNESS

Minor Lake

Consultation Lake

SEQUOIA NATIONAL PARK

Mount Whitney

Pinnacle Ridge

Wotans Throne

Mount Muir

Discovery Pinnacle

Climb onto a slight ledge and traverse to your right about 30 feet until a series of small flakes are met. From here, use this formation as a ladder to climb to the next ledge. Carefully pick your way through the ledges and cracks. You will encounter some exposure as you make the final moves to the summit. Even though the rock looks stable, always test it before putting your full weight and safety on the line. The tectonic activity in the region means that the stability of the ground is constantly changing.

Downclimb back to Trail Crest. Once you reach Trail Crest, you can head directly back down the Whitney Portal Trail to your vehicle.

Extended Route: John Muir Trail (Horseshoe Meadow)

Finding the trailhead: From Lone Pine, at the intersection of US 395 and Whitney Portal Road, head west (toward the mountains). At 3.2 miles, turn left (south) on Horseshoe Meadow Road. At 22.5 miles, turn right (north), following the sign to New Army Pass and Cottonwood Lakes. At 23 miles, arrive at the Cottonwood Lakes Trailhead. Park in a designated space and walk past the interpretive display to reach the trail. GPS: 36.52330°N / 118.238°W

With the daily access permits to the Whitney Portal Trail limited to 100, with some creativity and a few more miles underfoot you can still reach the summit. By initially entering Inyo National Forest and then Sequoia National Forest from either Horseshoe Meadow (Mount Langley) or from Shepards Pass (Mount Tyndall), your permit will allow you to summit Mount Muir and exit via the Whitney Portal Trail. The kicker to this workaround is that from Horseshoe Meadow, 21.7 miles are added to the trip. Entering from Shepards Pass increases the distance by 17.5 miles. These options are really only viable if you can arrange for transportation between the two trailheads unless you want to hike back to your starting point. Both of the routes also allow you to bag several fourteeners along the way.

From Horseshoe Meadow, this hike has a gradual elevation gain of only 4,000 feet. Leaving the parking area, it will take you almost 3 miles to gain 1,000 feet of elevation, making for a pleasant and nontechnical hike. The most popular, and the safest and easiest, route will be taking the Cottonwood Lakes Trail to the Old Army Pass Trail. You will find good footing and water sources along the trail. Depending on the time of year you are hiking, the meadows may be lush with wildflowers. Mount Langley will first come into view as the trail passes Cottonwood Lake #1. Continue on the Old Army Pass Trail around Cottonwood Lake #5, and you will find the steepest part of the hike. The trail snakes its way up a granite cliff, gaining more than 1,000 feet in just over a half mile. You may encounter some snow and/or ice on this section, as the cliff shades the trail from the sun. Depending on the conditions, it may be necessary to use crampons or micro-spikes to provide traction. Look closely and you just may see bighorn sheep watching your progress.

At the top of the ridge, Mount Langley sits directly to the north. To continue to Mount Whitney, continue down the trail heading west for 2.5 miles. When the T-intersection is reached, take the south branch for about a mile and you will junction with the Pacific Crest Trail (PCT). The PCT is well traveled and you will likely encounter through-hikers along the trail. At this point the PCT travels almost due west (to the right) and southeast (to the left). Continue up the "right" trail and it will gradually turn to the north.

Once on the PCT, the elevation will hover around 10,000 feet. The trail crosses several creeks and streams that run throughout the year. Be sure to treat or filter, or both, any water used for drinking and cooking since there is an abundance of wildlife around. Make sure to use your bear canister properly if you camp along the trail. There is a ranger station at Rock Creek, and they will check your permit. Keep on the PCT for another 5.5 miles until the trail meets the JMT at Crabtree Meadow. Head east at this point.

You will pass another ranger station at Crabtree. There are several dispersed campsites along the trail near Guitar Lake. Situated just below the series of switchbacks west of Trail Crest, this is a great area to rest up for your sunrise summit. Breaking camp early sets you up to watch the sun come up over the Owens Valley from the top of Mount Whitney. Take your time scaling the switchbacks. Depending on the season, you may encounter some snow or ice, making footing challenging. After gaining almost 2,000 vertical feet since leaving camp, you will step onto Trail Crest (13,484 feet) and the approach to Mount Muir will be about five minutes hiking to your north.

Often hikers will leave their backpacks on the side of the trail while they ascend the Class 3 scramble to the summit block. You may have to lean into the rock faces and use your hands to balance and traverse the route to the summit. Expect the final 600-vertical-foot climb to have a little exposure and take up to an hour to complete. As you begin the ascent from the JMT, expect to find some loose material. While not really scree, your footing may feel a bit unstable.

Climb onto a slight ledge and traverse to your right about 30 feet until a series of small flakes are met. From here, use this formation as a ladder to climb to the next ledge. Carefully pick your way through the ledges and cracks. You will encounter some exposure as you make the final moves to the summit. Even though the rock looks stable, always test it before putting your full weight and safety on the line. The tectonic activity in the region means that the stability of the ground is constantly changing.

Downclimb back to Trail Crest. Once you reach Trail Crest you can either continue on to Mount Whitney or, if arrangements have been made, you can head directly back down the Whitney Portal Trail to your car.

Even though you entered through Horseshoe Meadow, you can descend via the Whitney Portal Trail, or you can retrace your steps back to Horseshoe Meadow. From this point you can also continue on to summit Mount Whitney. Once you reach the top of the infamous 99 switchbacks below Trail Crest on the way to the trailhead, you will encounter fellow hikers on their way to the summit. Keep the Rules of the Trail in mind and allow the uphill climbers the right-of-way. Chances are they will wave

The geographic combination of the Eastern Sierra Mountains and the Owens Valley allows the creation of unique cloud formations like this lenticular cloud over Lone Pine.

you right on by, but give them the choice. There will not be a water source until you reach Trail Camp. From Trail Camp, the final few miles of trail wind down through the tree line and will spill you out onto the doorstep of the Whitney Portal Store.

Without having transportation at the base of the Whitney Portal Trail, simply retrace your steps back down the JMT and exit at Cottonwood Lakes.

Extended Route: Shepards Pass

Finding the trailhead: From Independence, at the intersection of US 395 and Market Street, go west toward the mountains on Market Street, which becomes Onion Valley Road. At 4.5 miles, turn left (south) onto Foothill Road. At 7.5 miles, bear left at the fork in the road, following the sign for the Shepards Pass Hiker Trail. In 8.4 miles, turn right (toward the mountains). At 9.2 miles, arrive at the Shepards Pass Trailhead. GPS: 36.65610°N / 118.3103°W

Accessing Mount Whitney from Shepards Pass provides a second alternative if you have been unable to secure a permit for the Whitney Portal Trail. Taking this route allows for the option to summit Mount Williamson, Mount Tyndall, Mount Barnard, and Mount Whitney in addition to Mount Muir. Trail conditions will vary greatly depending on the time of year you are climbing. During the winter and into late spring, you will likely encounter snow as low as Mahogany Flat and all the way to Shepards Pass and beyond. These conditions will require crampons or micro-spikes and an ice axe for safety. As the snow melts, the water level in Symmes Creek and Shepards Creek can become dangerously high. At various points the trail will traverse scree fields, making footing loose and slick during the early climbing period. Due to the steepness of the drainage that is home to Shepards Creek, down-mountain winds can blow hard and fast.

Water sources are abundant throughout the entire hike. In addition to Symmes Creek, the trail crosses several natural springs. At both Mahogany Flat and Anvil Camp, Shepards Creek is accessible. Water can also be found around the "Pothole." Once you crest Shepards Pass, Tyndall Creek and several tarns serve as water sources. Having so many water sources means that you can eliminate some weight in your pack by filling your bottle often. Remember that water will be the single heaviest item in your pack, but keep in mind that you need to stay hydrated to perform at your physical and mental best.

In the 10.5 miles from the trailhead to Shepards Pass, almost 8,000 feet of vertical await you. The trail climbs away from the Owens Valley and, just a few minutes later, crosses Symmes Creek for the first time. In the springtime the snowmelt water may reach knee height. While the water will be cold, the creek bottom is relatively smooth, so you could make this crossing barefoot. Otherwise, it is advisable to pack dry socks and footwear to prevent chafing and blisters later in the hike. During the summer months the creek can be crossed with ease and without submerging your feet. Depending on water levels, you will cross Symmes Creek two or three times within the first hour of hiking. Foot care is vital to a successful and enjoyable backcountry trip, so make sure that your feet are as dry as possible after crossing the creek.

Leaving Symmes Creek behind, the trail switchbacks its way toward Mahogany Flat, and in about 4 miles, Mount Williamson comes into view as you crest an unnamed pass. There are several protected campsites to the left of the trail. The trail drops away from the pass and crosses some scree fields and a small stream before climbing up to Mahogany Flat a mile or so later. At just under halfway to the pass, this is a popular place to camp. A trail leads down to the creek below to refill water if needed. In late May and early June, do not be surprised to find patches of snow as you begin to switchback up the trail below Mount Keith to the north. While the trail conditions may vary, the overall footing will be solid and without exposure.

Anvil Camp, right at the tree line, will be your next landmark. If you camp here, be mindful of the mosquitoes and blackflies during the warmer months. Above Anvil Camp, the boulder and talus fields of the Pothole begin. Late in the season, the trail will be clearly defined and easy to follow. In the spring, however, the conditions can be more challenging. Due to the sun protection created by the ridge to the south and the pass above, the final mile in distance and 1,000 feet in elevation gain up to Shepards Pass can be choked with snow during this period.

The approach from the Pacific Crest Trail/John Muir Trail passes by Guitar Lake. This water source serves as the overnight camp for many hikers on the way to Mount Whitney.

To successfully and safely reach the pass via a snow-covered trail, you will need to break out your ice axe and crampons. With parts of the trail covered with snow, traversing the talus field will be easier than hopping from rock to rock. Bear in mind that the trail, without snow cover, is very well defined and easy to follow all the way to the top of the pass. The trail will follow a series of switchbacks up the right side of the face, but when there are frozen conditions, those ice tools come in handy. Instead of hiking back and forth across the face on a dry trail, use your crampons to kick steps and move vertically up the final pitch to the top. Unless you are extremely comfortable with using an ice axe and wearing crampons, do not attempt to climb Shepards Pass under these conditions.

Once you reach the top of the pass, Mount Tyndall comes into view almost immediately to your southwest. Continue west on the trail through the valley for 3.5 miles. Several streams winding near the trail provide treatable water sources. At the Tyndall Creek junction, the trail you are on meets with the combined PCT and the JMT. A ranger station can also be found near this intersection. Take the PCT/JMT heading south for just over 7.5 miles. At this point the two trails separate and the JMT heads east toward the approach to Mount Whitney.

There are several dispersed campsites along the trail near Guitar Lake. Situated just below the series of switchbacks west of Trail Crest, this is a great area to rest up for your sunrise summit. Breaking camp early sets you up to watch the sun come up over the Owens Valley from the top of Mount Whitney. Take your time scaling the switchbacks. Depending on the season, you may encounter some snow or ice, making footing challenging. After gaining almost 2,000 vertical feet since leaving camp, you will step onto Trail Crest (13,484 feet) and Mount Whitney will be to your north.

Often hikers will leave their backpacks on the side of the trail while they ascend the Class 3 scramble to the summit block. You may have to lean into the rock faces and use your hands to balance and traverse the route to the summit. Expect the final 600-vertical-foot climb to have a little exposure and take up to an hour to complete. As you begin the ascent from the JMT, expect to find some loose material. While not really scree, your footing may feel a bit unstable.

Climb onto a slight ledge and traverse to your right about 30 feet until a series of small flakes are met. From here, use this formation as a ladder to climb to the next ledge. Carefully pick your way through the ledges and cracks. You will encounter some exposure as you make the final moves to the summit. Even though the rock looks stable, always test it before putting your full weight and safety on the line. The tectonic activity in the region means that the stability of the ground is constantly changing.

Downclimb back to the well-traveled Trail Crest. From this point you can easily continue on to Mount Whitney or head off the mountain. If you have made transportation arrangements, you can take the most direct route down the Whitney Portal Trail.

Even though you entered through Horseshoe Meadow, you can descend via the Whitney Portal Trail, or you can retrace your steps back to Horseshoe Meadow. Just before you reach the JMT junction, the summit approach for Mount Muir will be on your left. Once you reach the top of the infamous 99 switchbacks below Trail Crest on the way to the trailhead, you will encounter fellow hikers on their way to the summit. Keep the Rules of the Trail in mind and allow the uphill climbers the right-of-way. Chances are they will wave you right on by, but give them the choice. There will not be a water source until you reach Trail Camp. From Trail Camp, the final few miles of trail wind down through the tree line and will spill you out onto the doorstep of the Whitney Portal Store.

If your car remains at the Shepards Pass trailhead, you will simply return via the JMT. On this route you can also summit Mount Tyndall and Mount Williamson before reaching the trailhead.

Hiking Information

Closest Outfitters

Big Willi Mountaineering Company, 120 S. Main St., Ste. 13 and 14, Lone Pine, CA 93545; (760) 878-2849; https://bigwillimc.com

Stop in for last-minute supplies and ask Blair about his favorite places to explore in the Sierras. If you are driving north on US 395 from picking up your permit, Big Willi is located just past the stoplight in Lone Pine.

Whitney Portal Store, Whitney Portal Trailhead; (760) 876-0030; www.whitneyportalstore.com

Great Pre- or Post-Mountain Spots

Whitney Portal Store, Whitney Portal Trailhead; (760) 876-0030; www.whitneyportalstore.com

From its trailside location, the Whitney Portal Store serves up huge pancakes to fuel your climb, made-to-order burgers to reward success, cold beer to wash it all down with, and the most up-to-date trail and mountain conditions available. This family-owned store has been taking care of hiker needs for decades and offers live webcam views of Mount Whitney.

Mt. Whitney Restaurant, 227 S. Main St., Lone Pine, CA 93545; (760) 876-5751

Great place to fuel up before heading to any of the trailheads in the area. Over the years, Hollywood's stars have dined here while filming in the Alabama Hills.

Shuttle Service

Eastern Sierra Shuttle Service, Lone Pine, CA; info@mountwhitneyshuttle .com

On the way to Mount Langley the trail passes through meadows and around spring-fed lakes. Cottonwood Lake #5 serves as a reflecting pool for the mountains above just after sunrise.

3 Mount Whitney

Elevation: 14,505 feet, 1st highest
Start: Whitney Portal Trailhead
Distance: 22 miles round-trip
Primary route: Mount Whitney Trail
Elevation gain: 6,145 feet
Hiking time: 14 to 24+ hours
Difficulty: Class 1, Class 2
Trail surface: Dirt trail leading to talus and scree
Trailhead elevation: 8,360 feet
Camping: Designated campsites near trailhead, dispersed camping at Outpost Camp and Trail Camp

Fees: None
Permit: Yes
Best seasons: Summer and fall
Maps: Tom Harrison Mt. Whitney Zone, Mt. Whitney High Country; National Geographic #322: Mt. Whitney; Wilderness Press Mt. Whitney; USGS Mount Whitney
Nearest town: Lone Pine, CA
Trail contact: Mount Whitney Ranger District, PO Box 8, Lone Pine, CA 93545; (760) 876-6200
First ascent: August 18, 1873, Charles Begole, Albert Johnson, and John Lucas

Finding the trailhead: From Lone Pine, at the intersection of US 395 and Whitney Portal Road, head west (toward the mountains). In 13 miles, arrive at the Whitney Portal Trailhead parking area. GPS: 36.57860°N / 118.293°W

The Hike

The highest point in the lower 48 states reaches above the Owens Valley to the tune of 14,505 feet above sea level. More than 20,000 people attempt to reach its summit every year. Being granted a coveted permit through the lottery system that allows for 100 people a day on the trail feels like a nightclub velvet rope opening up. The scenery and vistas from the moment you leave the parking lot to the second you reach the summit are breathtaking. The main trail is easy to follow and reaches just Class 2 technical status during most of the year. Located just a few hours' drive from Los Angeles, Las Vegas, and San Francisco and with paved roads right to the trailhead, Mount Whitney is the most popular of the fourteeners in California. Bagging a second fourteener in Mount Muir on the same trip makes complete sense, as the approaches to both summits can be made from Trail Crest.

Most Popular Route: Whitney Portal Trail

Even though Mount Whitney may be easy to get to and, for much of the season, the route does not require serious mountaineering skills, many people arrive unprepared for the conditions on the mountain. Just over half of the people who attempt to climb the more than 6,000 feet of elevation over 11 miles fail to reach the summit. Lack of preparation, inadequate gear, and an overestimation of fitness level can bring you back to your vehicle feeling defeated. These three issues can also lead to a helicopter rescue off the mountain, debilitating injuries, and in extreme circumstances, death.

Once you leave Lone Pine, CA, for the trailhead, Mount Whitney comes into view over the Alabama Hills, giving you the first glimpse of her summit.

Mount Whitney looms above the drive into Whitney Portal, inviting you to climb to her top and enjoy the view from the tallest point in the lower 48 states. The effort and strength required to reach the summit will make signing the registry worth it.

Depending on the time of year, the existing snowpack may cover the switchbacks above Trail Camp and require the use of crampons and ice axes to gain the ridgeline.

Arriving at Whitney Portal with the right equipment and fitness level puts you ahead of the summit game. Knowing how your gear fits and works and where it is in your pack before setting out will increase your success level. Put in some training time prior to showing up at the trail. Constantly trekking uphill as the oxygen content of the air you are breathing diminishes will definitely stress your body.

Drink early and drink often. Staying hydrated is a vital part of your successful summit. In addition to starting out with bottles and hydration bladders full at the trailhead, several water sources can be found along the way up the mountain. You will cross the first creek within a few minutes on the trail. Just below the start of the 99 switchbacks, at Trail Camp, you will find the last consistent water source before the summit. As with all mountain streams, ponds, and lakes, it is wise to filter or purify all water used for drinking or cooking to protect yourself from bacteria.

The temperature and weather conditions can, and will, change dramatically as you make your way toward 14,505 feet. For every 1,000 feet in elevation you gain, 10 degrees in ambient temperature will be lost. An air temperature of 60 degrees F (15 degrees C) at the trailhead will become 40 degrees F (4 degrees C) at Outpost Camp and 20 degrees F (−6 degrees C) at Trail Camp. It will be even colder, and windy, at the summit. Having the right gear and layers will protect you from the elements all the way to the summit and back.

The most popular way to reach the summit successfully includes camping along the trail. Depending on the length of your permit, you will be assigned a campsite at one of two locations. Camp only in designated areas, and make sure to hang your food bag or canister at least 30 feet from your tent. At an elevation of 10,360 feet, Outpost Camp lies just over 3 miles from the trailhead. The trail to get to the camp is easy to follow and overnighting here will allow your body to acclimate slightly to the change in elevation. You will still find shade and cover from the forest at this elevation. For many people, this is a perfect day one stopping point.

Three more miles (and approximately another 2,000 feet) up lies Trail Camp. Those looking for a two-day summit attempt will choose to bivy at this higher camp at the end of the first day. Reaching this location will take several hours for most people, and the luxury of stretching out and relaxing before the final summit push will be welcome. Situated above the tree line, Trail Camp does not offer much in the way of protection from the sun, so choose your spot wisely. The camp lies just below the start of Whitney's infamous 99 switchbacks, so you can get a look at the 2 miles of granite trail waiting for you.

For a variety of reasons, it is smart to get an early start on your summit push. Once you start the next section of the hike, there will not be any consistent protection from the sun that beats down on the trail. Leaving at a predawn hour will eliminate most of the blazing sun on the way up. Since the trail traffic is regulated by permits, starting early will help avoid getting caught behind slower groups on the trail. Thunderstorms

Some of the most captivating views from Trail Crest to the summit of Whitney will be to the west. The reflection of Hitchcock Mountain in the Hitchcock Lakes below is just one example. From this point you will also be able to see the John Muir Trail snaking its way up the mountain to join you.

can arrive without much advance warning in the afternoon. Getting caught on an exposed ridge in a lightning storm will potentially result in serious injury, so plan to be down before afternoon.

Mentally, there is an advantage to leaving in the dark. The actual hiking distance from Trail Camp to Trail Crest on the switchbacks is 2.2 miles. The direct distance is about half of that, which means that in roughly 1 mile the elevation changes 1,140 feet. The switchbacks meander up the cliff face at a pitch that most can hike with relative ease. Traversing back and forth every few minutes, the pass at Trail Crest pops in and out of view. It becomes easy to look too far ahead and feel like the progress being made is not much progress at all. Leaving Trail Camp while it is still dark eliminates the ability to look too far up the trail. You can only focus on the trail that your headlamp illuminates right in front of you. Looking up, Trail Crest will not be visible. Looking down will reveal the headlamps of other climbers on the trail behind you. This section can be a bottleneck, as the travel pace will be relatively slow.

In the spring, early summer, and late fall, you may encounter snow and ice covering the trail above the tree line. Travel from Trail Camp to Trail Crest will not utilize the famous switchbacks; rather, you will use your crampons and ice axe to traverse the chute. An understanding of how these pieces of equipment should be used is necessary before showing up at the trailhead. Make sure your ice axe has a leash so that it does not slide away from you if it falls. Always keep your axe in your uphill hand. Practice self-arrest techniques with the ice axe so that you can react quickly should you start to slide down the mountain. Your ice axe can save you from injury or worse. Crampons provide an additional level of traction while walking on frozen surfaces. Please seek instruction from a trained professional on how to use these ice tools.

If you do not possess the skills to competently use an ice axe and crampons, *do not* attempt to climb the chute to Trail Crest. You should call ahead for current weather conditions to be prepared. Due to the lottery system for Mount Whitney permits, many people approach the mountain without taking the trail conditions into consideration, feeling that since they "won" a permit, they have to attempt the climb. Summit fever can be a dangerous thing. While dehydration and altitude sickness commonly occur when the trail is clear, the consequences are far greater when snow and ice are present.

Without adequate training and skills with both crampons and ice axe, you will endanger not only yourself but those around you as well. The physical exertion of climbing combined with the unpredictable footing that ice and snow provide can lead to slips and falls. Falls of this nature can go for hundreds of feet, resulting in injury, rescue, and, in extreme cases, death. Be mindful of your party's skill set if you encounter frozen conditions. The mountain will always be there, and you can always try again if the danger level seems high.

The real reason to break Trail Camp and start up the route while it is still dark out is so that you can watch the sun rise from the highest point in the lower 48 states!

Once you reach Trail Crest, there will be just 2 more miles and less than 900 feet to climb. This last section provides the most exposure as you traverse the ridgeline. There are some very steep drop-offs on both sides of the trail, so be mindful of where your feet go. The John Muir Trail (JMT) climbs up from the west and intersects with the Whitney approach about a half mile past Trail Crest. Do not be alarmed if you see backpacks lying trailside in this area. Commonly there will be through-hikers along this section, and since the JMT finishes at Whitney Portal, they will drop their packs and summit Whitney before descending the trail. It is also important to note that just a few minutes' hiking past this trail intersection will be the approach to Mount Muir.

The only thing lying between you and the summit at this point is a boulder field that may require a little bit of scrambling to get through. The true summit lies east of the old Smithsonian Institution Shelter, or Mount Whitney Hut. The small hut offers some protection from the elements but is not intended for overnight camping. Follow the same route back to the trailhead. Do not forget to bag Mount Muir on the way down. Celebrate your successful trip with a burger from the Whitney Portal Store!

Mountaineer's Route

What is now called the Mountaineer's Route was first used to reach the Mount Whitney summit by John Muir in 1873. This route is the most direct to the actual summit but will require a higher skill level than the main trail does. The latter sections of this hike will require route-finding skills, as the trail is unmaintained. You will also find some Class 2/3 scrambling sections as the summit is approached. In late spring it will not be unusual to encounter sections of snow and ice above 12,000 feet, so pack your ice axe and crampons. Always check the trail conditions prior to hitting the trail.

Since the "trail" referred to as the Mountaineer's Route is not maintained by the National Forest Service, hikers should be prepared to navigate their way. Even if you choose to use a GPS unit, it is suggested to always pack a map and compass as a backup. Much like the more popular Whitney Portal Trail ascent, this route can be broken up into a multiday trip or done as one long up-and-back.

Starting just steps from the Whitney Portal Store, the hike to Mount Whitney follows the Whitney Portal Trail for about a mile before you bear right onto the North Fork Lone Pine Creek Trail. Look for the wooden sign that says North Fork (Lone Pine Creek). Head uphill with the creek on your right side and you will find a well-defined and -maintained trail. The trail crosses to the north side of the creek and leads you to a granite cliff face. At this point expect the trail to be difficult to follow at times.

Maintain the north side of the creek for just over a quarter mile of distance. Your waypoint will be the large "Matterhorn" rock formation. Once you reach the way-point, scramble your way onto the Ebersbacher Ledges above you. Continue to work through the steep ledges east and then west as you gain elevation. Take your time and watch where you place your feet. Once you have reached the top ledge, hike around

Mount Whitney and Mount Muir: Mountaineer's Route

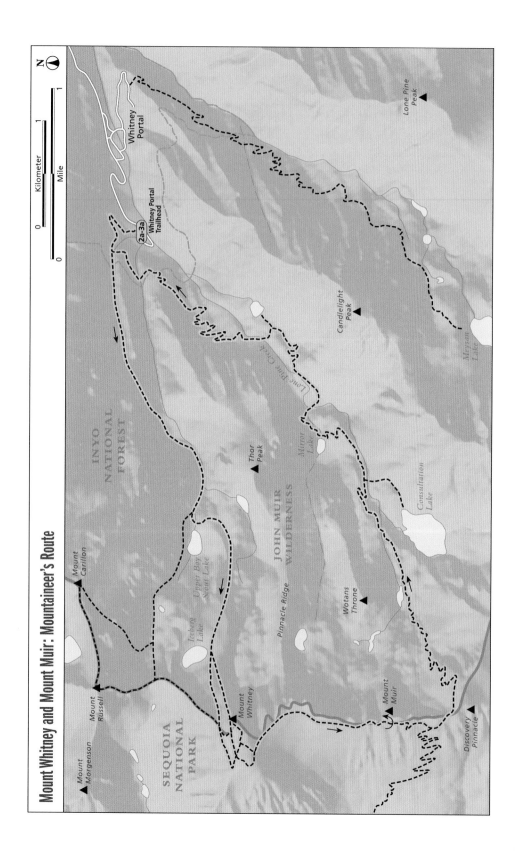

the base of the granite cliff until Lower Boy Scout Lake is reached. While only a short distance into the hike, campsites can be found here.

From Lower Boy Scout Lake to Upper Boy Scout Lake, maintaining your route can become challenging. You will encounter several trail options. Take the trail found just above the willow trees. You may encounter route cairns that will help guide you through the talus and rocky slabs that lie between the two lakes. The distance from the trailhead to Upper Boy Scout Lake will be just a shade over 3.5 miles. Avoid bushwhacking through the willow trees and undergrowth. If you are planning on making this a multiday trip, set up camp here. This location also makes a great approach point to Mount Russell.

Leaving Upper Boy Scout Lake with 2.5 miles remaining to the summit of Mount Whitney, the trail crosses through a glacial moraine. Once you reach the top of the moraine, the trail heads toward the creek. Depending on the time of year, you may pass a waterfall and find water seeping from the cliffside. Continue west until you encounter a break in the cliff that will allow you to scramble up through scree and some ledges. Since there may be some water crossings in this steep section, be mindful that your feet may slip on the rocks due to wet shoes.

Work your way up the trail until you reach Iceberg Lake. Mount Whitney will be directly above you. The Mountaineer's Route follows the large gully visible to the right (north) of Mount Whitney. Depending on the time of year and the winter snowpack, you may need to use crampons and an ice axe to make your way up this couloir. If snow can be avoided, there is an abundance of solid hand- and footholds for use. At just over 14,000 feet you reach the notch at the top of the couloir. Mount Russell's east ridge approach can be made from this point.

From the notch, drop down to the water-stained gully to your left. Once in the gully, ascend using the ledges on both sides to climb the final few hundred feet to the summit. To descend, follow the Whitney Portal Trail. Make sure to summit Mount Muir on the way down.

Extended Route: John Muir Trail (Horseshoe Meadow)

Finding the trailhead: From Lone Pine, at the intersection of US 395 and Whitney Portal Road, head west (toward the mountains). At 3.2 miles, turn left (south) on Horseshoe Meadow Road. At 22.5 miles, turn right (north), following the sign to New Army Pass and Cottonwood Lakes. At 23 miles, arrive at the Cottonwood Lakes Trailhead. Park in a designated space and walk past the interpretive display to reach the trail. GPS: 36.52330°N / 118.238°W

With the daily access permits to the Whitney Portal Trail limited to 100, with some creativity and a few more miles underfoot you can still reach the summit. By initially entering Inyo National Forest and then Sequoia National Forest from either Horseshoe Meadow (Mount Langley) or from Shepards Pass (Mount Tyndall), your permit will allow you to summit Mount Whitney and exit via the Whitney Portal Trail. The kicker to this workaround is that from Horseshoe Meadow, 21.7 miles are added

Leaving Trail Camp and ascending the switchbacks in the dark will allow you to welcome the sunrise from the summit of Mount Whitney.

to the trip. Entering from Shepards Pass increases the distance by 17.5 miles. These options are really only viable if you can arrange for transportation between the two trailheads unless you want to hike back to your starting point. Both of the routes also allow you to bag several fourteeners along the way.

From Horseshoe Meadow, this hike has a gradual elevation gain of only 4,000 feet. Leaving the parking area, it will take you almost 3 miles to gain 1,000 feet of elevation, making for a pleasant and nontechnical hike. The most popular, and the safest and easiest, route will be taking the Cottonwood Lakes Trail to the Old Army Pass Trail. You will find good footing and water sources along the trail. Depending on the time of year you are hiking, the meadows may be lush with wildflowers. Mount Langley will first come into view as the trail passes Cottonwood Lake #1. Continue on the Old Army Pass Trail around Cottonwood Lake #5, and you will find the steepest part of the hike. The trail snakes its way up a granite cliff, gaining more than 1,000 feet in just over a half mile. You may encounter some snow and/or ice on this section, as the cliff shades the trail from the sun. Depending on the conditions, it may be necessary to use crampons or micro-spikes to provide traction. Look closely and you just may see bighorn sheep watching your progress.

At the top of the ridge, Mount Langley sits directly to the north. To continue to Mount Whitney, continue down the trail heading west for 2.5 miles. When the T-intersection is reached, take the south branch for about a mile and you will junction with the Pacific Crest Trail (PCT). The PCT is well traveled and you will likely encounter through-hikers along the trail. At this point the PCT travels almost due west (to the right) and southeast (to the left). Continue up the "right" trail and it will gradually turn to the north.

Once on the PCT, the elevation will hover around 10,000 feet. The trail crosses several creeks and streams that run throughout the year. Be sure to treat or filter, or both, any water used for drinking and cooking since there is an abundance of wildlife around. Make sure to use your bear canister properly if you camp along the trail. There is a ranger station at Rock Creek, and they will check your permit. Keep on the PCT for another 5.5 miles until the trail meets the JMT at Crabtree Meadow. Head east at this point.

You will pass another ranger station at Crabtree. There are several dispersed campsites along the trail near Guitar Lake. Situated just below the series of switchbacks west of Trail Crest, this is a great area to rest up for your sunrise summit. Breaking camp early sets you up to watch the sun come up over the Owens Valley from the top of Mount Whitney. Take your time scaling the switchbacks. Depending on the season, you may encounter some snow or ice, making footing challenging. After gaining almost 2,000 vertical feet since leaving camp, you will step onto Trail Crest (13,484 feet) and Mount Whitney will be to your north. Depending on the weather conditions, it is not uncommon for hikers to leave their packs beside the trail just after the JMT reaches the ridgeline. If you choose to do this, make sure to take water, food, and an extra layer with you to the summit.

Once you reach Trail Crest, there will be just 1.5 more miles and less than 800 feet to climb. This last section provides the most exposure as you traverse the ridge-line. There are some very steep drop-offs on both sides of the trail, so be mindful of where your feet go. The only thing lying between you and the summit at this point is a boulder field that may require a little bit of scrambling to get through. The true summit lies east of the old Smithsonian Institution Shelter, or Mount Whitney Hut. The small hut offers some protection from the elements but is not intended for over-night camping.

Even though you entered through Horseshoe Meadow, you can descend via the Whitney Portal Trail, or you can retrace your steps back to Horseshoe Meadow. Just before you reach the JMT junction, the summit approach for Mount Muir will be on your left. Once you reach the top of the infamous 99 switchbacks below Trail Crest on the way to the trailhead, you will encounter fellow hikers on their way to the summit. Keep the Rules of the Trail in mind and allow the uphill climbers the right-of-way. Chances are they will wave you right on by, but give them the choice. There will not be a water source until you reach Trail Camp. From Trail Camp, the final few miles of trail wind down through the tree line and will spill you out onto the doorstep of the Whitney Portal Store.

Extended Route: Shepards Pass

Finding the trailhead: From Independence, at the intersection of US 395 and Market Street, go west toward the mountains on Market Street, which becomes Onion Valley Road. At 4.5 miles, turn left (south) onto Foothill Road. At 7.5 miles, bear left at the fork in the road, following the sign for the Shepards Pass Hiker Trail. In 8.4 miles, turn right (toward the mountains). At 9.2 miles, arrive at the Shepards Pass Trailhead. GPS: 36.65610°N / 118.3103°W

Accessing Mount Whitney from Shepards Pass provides a second alternative if you have been unable to secure a permit for the Whitney Portal Trail. Taking this route allows for the option to summit Mount Williamson, Mount Tyndall, Mount Barnard, and Mount Muir in addition to Mount Whitney. Trail conditions will vary greatly depending on the time of year you are climbing. During the winter and into late spring, you will likely encounter snow as low as Mahogany Flat and all the way to Shepards Pass and beyond. These conditions will require crampons or micro-spikes and an ice axe for safety. As the snow melts, the water level in Symmes Creek and Shepards Creek can become dangerously high. At various points the trail will traverse scree fields, making footing loose and slick during the early climbing period. Due to the steepness of the drainage that is home to Shepards Creek, down-mountain winds can blow hard and fast.

Water sources are abundant throughout the entire hike. In addition to Symmes Creek, the trail crosses several natural springs. At both Mahogany Flat and Anvil Camp, Shepards Creek is accessible. Water can also be found around the "Pothole." Once you crest Shepards Pass, Tyndall Creek and several tarns serve as water sources. Having so many water sources means that you can eliminate some weight in your pack by filling your bottle often. Remember that water will be the single heaviest item in your pack, but keep in mind that you need to stay hydrated to perform at your physical and mental best.

In the 10.5 miles from the trailhead to Shepards Pass, almost 8,000 feet of vertical await you. The trail climbs away from the Owens Valley and, just a few minutes later, crosses Symmes Creek for the first time. In the springtime the snowmelt water may reach knee height. While the water will be cold, the creek bottom is relatively smooth, so you could make this crossing barefoot. Otherwise, it is advisable to pack dry socks and footwear to prevent chafing and blisters later in the hike. During the summer months the creek can be crossed with ease and without submerging your feet. Depending on water levels, you will cross Symmes Creek two or three times within the first hour of hiking. Foot care is vital to a successful and enjoyable backcountry trip, so make sure that your feet are as dry as possible after crossing the creek.

Leaving Symmes Creek behind, the trail switchbacks its way toward Mahogany Flat, and in about 4 miles, Mount Williamson comes into view as you crest an unnamed pass. There are several protected campsites to the left of the trail. The trail drops away from the pass and crosses some scree fields and a small stream before climbing up to Mahogany Flat a mile or so later. At just under halfway to the pass, this is a popular place to camp. A trail leads down to the creek below to refill water if needed. In late May and early June, do not be surprised to find patches of snow as you begin to switchback up the trail below Mount Keith to the north. While the trail conditions may vary, the overall footing will be solid and without exposure.

Anvil Camp, right at the tree line, will be your next landmark. If you camp here, be mindful of the mosquitoes and blackflies during the warmer months. Above Anvil Camp, the boulder and talus fields of the Pothole begin. Late in the season, the trail will be clearly defined and easy to follow. In the spring, however, the conditions can be more challenging. Due to the sun protection created by the ridge to the south and the pass above, the final mile in distance and 1,000 feet in elevation gain up to Shepards Pass can be choked with snow during this period.

To successfully and safely reach the pass via a snow-covered trail, you will need to break out your ice axe and crampons. With parts of the trail covered with snow, traversing the talus field will be easier than hopping from rock to rock. Bear in mind that the trail, without snow cover, is very well defined and easy to follow all the way to the top of the pass. The trail will follow a series of switchbacks up the right side of the face, but when there are frozen conditions, those ice tools come in handy. Instead

Just outside of Lone Pine on the way to Whitney Portal, the road will take you through the famous Alabama Hills. This area has served as the backdrop for movies and television shows since the 1920s. The blockbuster movies *Gladiator*, *Ironman*, and *Django Unchained* and more than 100 Westerns have been shot in this area. Dispersed camping is also allowed in the Alabama Hills.

To be standing on the highest spot in the lower 48 at any time of day is exhilarating, but timing your summit attempt to coincide with the sunrise over the valley below will take your breath away. Leave Trail Camp early enough, and this view will greet you at 14,505 feet.

of hiking back and forth across the face on a dry trail, use your crampons to kick steps and move vertically up the final pitch to the top. Unless you are extremely comfortable with using an ice axe and wearing crampons, do not attempt to climb Shepards Pass under these conditions.

Once you reach the top of the pass, Mount Tyndall comes into view almost immediately to your southwest. Continue west on the trail through the valley for 3.5 miles. Several streams winding near the trail provide treatable water sources. At the Tyndall Creek junction, the trail you are on meets with the combined PCT and the JMT. A ranger station can also be found near this intersection. Take the PCT/JMT heading south for just over 7.5 miles. At this point the two trails separate and the JMT heads east toward the approach to Mount Whitney.

There are several dispersed campsites along the trail near Guitar Lake. Situated just below the series of switchbacks west of Trail Crest, this is a great area to rest up for your sunrise summit. Breaking camp early sets you up to watch the sun come up over the Owens Valley from the top of Mount Whitney. Take your time scaling the switchbacks. Depending on the season, you may encounter some snow or ice, making footing challenging. After gaining almost 2,000 vertical feet since leaving camp, you will step onto Trail Crest (13,484 feet) and Mount Whitney will be to your north. Depending on the weather conditions, it is not uncommon for hikers to leave their packs beside the trail just after the JMT reaches the ridgeline. If you choose to do this, make sure to take water, food, and an extra layer with you to the summit.

Driving to the trailhead from Lone Pine, the Alabama Hills will be on the right side of the road. Many people take advantage of the dispersed camping opportunities here before heading up the Whitney Portal Trail. More than 300 movies have been filmed in this area, including Gladiator and Ironman. Hike the Arch Trail at the end of Movie Road to re-create the cover photo of this book.

Once you reach Trail Crest, there will be just 1.5 more miles and less than 800 feet to climb. This last section provides the most exposure as you traverse the ridge-line. There are some very steep drop-offs on both sides of the trail, so be mindful of where your feet go. The only thing lying between you and the summit at this point is a boulder field that may require a little bit of scrambling to get through. The true summit lies east of the old Smithsonian Institution Shelter, or Mount Whitney Hut. The small hut offers some protection from the elements but is not intended for overnight camping.

Even though you entered through Horseshoe Meadow, you can descend via the Whitney Portal Trail, or you can retrace your steps back to Horseshoe Meadow. Just before you reach the JMT junction, the summit approach for Mount Muir will be on your left. Once you reach the top of the infamous 99 switchbacks below Trail Crest on the way to the trailhead, you will encounter fellow hikers on their way to the summit. Keep the Rules of the Trail in mind and allow the uphill climbers the right-of-way. Chances are they will wave you right on by, but give them the choice. There will not be a water source until you reach Trail Camp. From Trail Camp, the final few miles of trail wind down through the tree line and will spill you out onto the doorstep of the Whitney Portal Store.

Hiking Information

Closest Outfitters

Big Willi Mountaineering Company, 120 S. Main St., Ste. 13 and 14, Lone Pine, CA 93545; (760) 878-2849; https://bigwillimc.com

Stop in for last-minute supplies and ask Blair about his favorite places to explore in the Sierras. If you are driving north on US 395 from picking up your permit, Big Willi is located just past the stoplight in Lone Pine.

Whitney Portal Store, Whitney Portal Trailhead; (760) 876-0030; www.whitney portalstore.com

Great Pre- or Post-Mountain Spots

Whitney Portal Store, Whitney Portal Trailhead; (760) 876-0030; www.whitney portalstore.com

From its trailside location, the Whitney Portal Store serves up huge pancakes to fuel your climb, made-to-order burgers to reward success, cold beer to wash it all down with, and the most up-to-date trail and mountain conditions available. This family-owned store has been taking care of hiker needs for decades and offers live webcam views of Mount Whitney.

Mt. Whitney Restaurant, 227 S. Main St., Lone Pine, CA 93545; (760) 876-5751

Great place to fuel up before heading to any of the trailheads in the area. Over the years, Hollywood's stars have dined here while filming in the Alabama Hills.

Shuttle Service

Eastern Sierra Shuttle Service, Lone Pine, CA; info@mountwhitneyshuttle .com

4 Mount Russell

Elevation: 14,088 feet, 10th highest
Start: Whitney Portal Trailhead
Distance: 8 miles round-trip
Primary route: Mount Whitney Trail to Mountaineer's Route to East Ridge
Elevation gain: 5,728 feet
Hiking time: 14 to 20 hours
Difficulty: Class 1, Class 3
Trail surface: Dirt trail leading to scree/talus, low-exposure scramble
Trailhead elevation: 8,360 feet
Camping: Designated campsites near trailhead, dispersed camping below Mount Carillon

Fees: None
Permit: Yes
Best seasons: Summer and fall; technical winter climb
Maps: Tom Harrison Mt. Whitney Zone, Mt. Whitney High Country; National Geographic #322: Mt. Whitney; Wilderness Press Mt. Whitney; USGS Mount Whitney
Nearest town: Lone Pine, CA
Trail contact: Mount Whitney Ranger District, PO Box 8, Lone Pine, CA 93545; (760) 876-6200
First ascent: June 24, 1926, Norman Clyde

Finding the trailhead: From Lone Pine, at the intersection of US 395 and Whitney Portal Road, head west (toward the mountains). In 13 miles, arrive at the Whitney Portal Trailhead parking area. GPS: 36.57860°N / 118.293°W

The Hike

As the crow flies, Mount Russell lies about a mile away from, and even shares a trailhead with, the more popular Mount Whitney and Mount Muir yet goes unnoticed by many of the area's visitors. The east ridge was first climbed by Norman Clyde and had become the most popular route to the summit. You can reach Mount Russell directly from Mount Whitney by traversing the Whitney-Russell saddle to combine three fourteeners in one trip. The east ridge, however, does not require the same level of mountaineering skill.

Since Mount Russell falls within the borders of the Whitney Zone, you will have to obtain a special permit to leave Whitney Portal. If so desired, you can structure your permit to allow the summit of Mount Russell and then a traverse to Mount Whitney and an exit down the main Whitney Portal Trail. You cannot, however, hike up to the summit of Mount Whitney first with this permit (see "Mount Whitney Permit Lottery Process" in the introduction). Make sure to have your permit with you at all times, as rangers will conduct spot checks on the trail. Always carry a map with you—staying oriented in the map and real world will keep you on the trail.

Comparable to climbing today, Clyde recounted the conditions of his first summit in the 1927 *Sierra Club Bulletin*:

> The route ahead looked formidable, at times impossible. To the south the wall
> dropped abruptly; to the north, after descending at a steep angle for few feet,

it fell away sheer. Difficult as it seemed from a distance, nevertheless the way opened up as I progressed. There was always a safe passage and there was always enough protuberances and crevices to afford secure handholds and footholds.

Now and then I came to a gash in the ridge through which I looked with a thrill down vertical cliffs, hundreds of feet in height, to the basin below and beyond to the flanks of Mt. Whitney. After reaching the end of a ledge, a short scramble brought me to the eastern summit of the mountain.

East Ridge Route

Starting just steps from the Whitney Portal Store, the hike to Mount Russell follows the Whitney Portal Trail for about a mile before you bear right onto the North Fork Lone Pine Creek Trail. Look for the wooden sign that says North Fork. Head uphill with the creek on your right side and you will find a well-defined and -maintained trail. The trail crosses the North Fork and leads you to a granite cliff face. Do not take the trail going left. The better route continues right, away from the cliff and back over the creek.

This trail continues for a couple of miles before the Ebersbacher Ledges appear on your right. The "E Ledges" will prove to be a very short Class 3 section as you follow the cairns back and forth across the ledges until you end up back on the trail heading west toward Lower Boy Scout Lake. Mount Whitney makes an appearance in the distance as you approach the lake and the talus field around it. At Upper Boy Scout Lake, take advantage of the stream crossing to fill up with water, as this will be the last source before the summit. Follow the trail along the creek feeding Upper Boy Scout Lake, heading north toward a hill.

Above (north/northwest), you will see a scree and sand hill. The Class 2 climbing up the scree can be a slippery challenge, as the surface can slip underfoot. You will be able to follow in the footsteps of climbers who have come before on the scree sections. The sand will slow your progress down, but eventually the saddle between Russell and Carillon will be reached. Do not get discouraged by the one-step-forward-two-steps-back mental grind of this section. Frustration just becomes wasted energy.

Once you gain the saddle, Mount Russell stands right in front of you. Walk the short distance to the start of the east ridge where the route is worn and defined. Scramble over the first little bit; there will be some exposure but the moves are pretty straightforward. The route follows the north side of the ridge for much of the remaining climb. If you are climbing in the early season when snow and ice are present, hiking up the crest, even with its greater level of exposure, will be the safer route. North of the ridge you will encounter a gully just before the lower east summit. Continue along the crest and past a small saddle.

To reach the true summit from this point, you will have to traverse a series of ledges on the north side of the ridge. When you are directly below the summit block, climb the blocks and ledges to the peak. This Class 3 section does have some exposure, but the moves are not too difficult. The summit block provides an amazing view of Mount Whitney and Mount Muir to the south and on a clear day Mount

Mount Russell

Williamson to the north. The Alabama Hills and Lone Pine will be off to the east in the valley below. Descend by retracing your footsteps back to Whitney Portal.

Mountaineer's Route

What is now called the Mountaineer's Route was first used to reach the Mount Whitney summit by John Muir in 1873. This route is the most direct to Whitney's actual summit but will require a higher skill level than the main trail does. The latter sections of this hike will require route-finding skills, as the trail is unmaintained. You will also find some Class 2/3 scrambling sections as the summit is approached. In late spring it will not be unusual to encounter sections of snow and ice above 12,000 feet, so pack your ice axe and crampons. Always check the trail conditions prior to hitting the trail.

Since the "trail" referred to as the Mountaineer's Route is not maintained by the National Forest Service, hikers should be prepared to navigate their way. Even if you choose to use a GPS unit, it is suggested to always pack a map and compass as a backup. Much like the more popular Whitney Portal Trail ascent, this route can be broken up into a multiday trip or done as one long up-and-back.

Starting just steps from the Whitney Portal Store, the hike to Mount Russell follows the Whitney Portal Trail for about a mile before you bear right onto the North Fork Lone Pine Creek Trail. Look for the wooden sign that says North Fork (Lone Pine Creek). Head uphill with the creek on your right side and you will find a well-defined and -maintained trail. The trail crosses to the north side of the creek and leads you to a granite cliff face. At this point expect the trail to be difficult to follow at times.

Maintain the north side of the creek for just over a quarter mile of distance. Your waypoint will be the large "Matterhorn" rock formation. Once you reach the waypoint, scramble your way onto the Ebersbacher Ledges above you. Continue to work through the steep ledges east and then west as you gain elevation. Take your time and watch where you place your feet. Once you have reached the top ledge, hike around the base of the granite cliff until Lower Boy Scout Lake is reached. While only a short distance into the hike, campsites can be found here.

From Lower Boy Scout Lake to Upper Boy Scout Lake, maintaining your route can become challenging. You will encounter several trail options. Take the trail found just above the willow trees. You may encounter route cairns that will help guide you through the talus and rocky slabs that lie between the two lakes. The distance from the trailhead to Upper Boy Scout Lake will be just a shade over 3.5 miles. Avoid bushwhacking through the willow trees and undergrowth. If you are planning on making this a multiday trip, set up camp here. This location also makes a great approach point to Mount Russell.

Above (north/northwest), you will see a scree and sand hill. The Class 2 climbing up the scree can be a slippery challenge, as the surface can slip underfoot. You will be able to follow in the footsteps of climbers who have come before on the scree sections. The sand will slow your progress down, but eventually the saddle between Russell and Carillon will be reached. Do not get discouraged by the one-step-forward-two-steps-back mental grind of this section. Frustration just becomes wasted energy.

Once you gain the saddle, Mount Russell stands right in front of you. Walk the short distance to the start of the east ridge where the route is worn and defined. Scramble over the first little bit; there will be some exposure but the moves are pretty straightforward. The route follows the north side of the ridge for much of the remaining climb. If you are climbing in the early season when snow and ice are present, hiking up the crest, even with its greater level of exposure, will be the safer route. North of the ridge you will encounter a gully just before the lower east summit. Continue along the crest and past a small saddle.

To reach the true summit from this point, you will have to traverse a series of ledges on the north side of the ridge. When you are directly below the summit block, climb the blocks and ledges to the peak. This Class 3 section does have some exposure, but the moves are not too difficult. The summit block provides an amazing view of Mount Whitney and Mount Muir to the south and on a clear day Mount Williamson to the north. The Alabama Hills and Lone Pine will be off to the east in the valley below.

Descend by carefully retracing your steps back to Upper Boy Scout Lake. Keep just above the willow trees and undergrowth along the unmaintained trail and navigate through the Ebersbacher Ledges to reach the North Fork Lone Pine Creek. Follow the trail until it joins the Whitney Portal Trail. Just a few minutes farther down the trail, and you will reach the parking lot.

Expanded Route: Traverse from Mount Whitney to Mountaineer's Route

With the relative summit proximity of Mount Russell and Mount Whitney, climbing both mountains, as well as Mount Muir, becomes a very viable option for those looking to maximize trail time and peak bag. You must have either a one-day or overnight permit granting access to the Whitney Portal Trail. Initial trail access to both mountains (as well as Mount Muir) starts just outside of the Whitney Portal Store.

By staying on the Whitney Portal Trail, the hike passes the approach to Mount Muir and goes directly to the summit of Mount Whitney. Combining these three mountains in one hike requires some additional planning, time, endurance, and skills.

Drink early and drink often. Staying hydrated is a vital part of your successful summit. In addition to starting out with bottles and hydration bladders full at the trailhead, several water sources can be found along the way up the mountain. You will cross the first creek within a few minutes on the trail. Just below the start of the 99 switchbacks, at Trail Camp, you will find the last consistent water source before the summit. As with all mountain streams, ponds, and lakes, it is wise to filter or purify all water used for drinking or cooking to protect yourself from bacteria.

The temperature and weather conditions can, and will, change dramatically as you make your way to higher elevations. For every 1,000 feet in elevation you gain, 10 degrees in ambient temperature will be lost. An air temperature of 60 degrees F (15 degrees C) at the trailhead will become 40 degrees F (4 degrees C) at Outpost Camp and 20 degrees F (−6 degrees C) at Trail Camp. It will be even colder, and windy, at the summit. Having the right gear and layers will protect you from the elements.

If you are planning on summiting Mount Whitney and then traversing to Mount Russell, the smart plan will be to camp along the way. Trail Camp lies just below the start of Whitney's infamous 99 switchbacks, so you can get a look at the 2 miles of granite trail waiting for you. There are plenty of dispersed camping sites located here. The last fresh water supply before the summit can also be found here.

For a variety of reasons, it is smart to get an early start on your summit push. Once you start the next section of the hike, there will not be any consistent protection from the sun that beats down on the trail. Leaving at a predawn hour will eliminate most of the blazing sun on the way up. Since the trail traffic is regulated by permits, starting early will also help avoid getting caught behind slower groups on the trail. Thunderstorms can arrive without much advance warning in the afternoon. Getting caught on an exposed ridge in a lightning storm will potentially result in serious injury, so plan to be down before afternoon.

Mentally, there is an advantage to leaving in the dark. The actual hiking distance from Trail Camp to Trail Crest on the switchbacks is 2.2 miles. The direct distance is about half of that, which means that in roughly 1 mile the elevation changes 1,140 feet. The switchbacks meander up the cliff face at a pitch that most can hike with relative ease. Traversing back and forth every few minutes, the pass at Trail Crest pops in and out of view. It becomes easy to look too far ahead and feel like the progress being made is not much progress at all. Leaving Trail Camp while it is still dark eliminates the ability to look too far up the trail. You can only focus on the trail that your headlamp illuminates right in front of you. Looking up, Trail Crest will not be visible. Looking down will reveal the headlamps of other climbers on the trail behind you. This section can be a bottleneck, as the travel pace will be relatively slow.

In the spring, early summer, and late fall, you may encounter snow and ice covering the trail above the tree line. Travel from Trail Camp to Trail Crest will not utilize the famous switchbacks; rather, you will use your crampons and ice axe to traverse the chute. An understanding of how these pieces of equipment should be used is necessary before showing up at the trailhead. Make sure your ice axe has a leash so that it does not slide away from you if it falls. Always keep your axe in your uphill hand. Practice self-arrest techniques with the ice axe so that you can react quickly should you start to slide down the mountain. Your ice axe can save you from injury or worse. Crampons provide an additional level of traction while walking on frozen surfaces. Please seek instruction from a trained professional on how to use these ice tools.

If you do not possess the skills to competently use an ice axe and crampons, *do not* attempt to climb the chute to Trail Crest. You should call ahead for current weather conditions to be prepared. Due to the lottery system for Mount Whitney permits, many people approach the mountain without taking the trail conditions into consideration, feeling that since they "won" a permit, they have to attempt the climb. Summit fever can be a dangerous thing. While dehydration and altitude sickness

Mount Russell

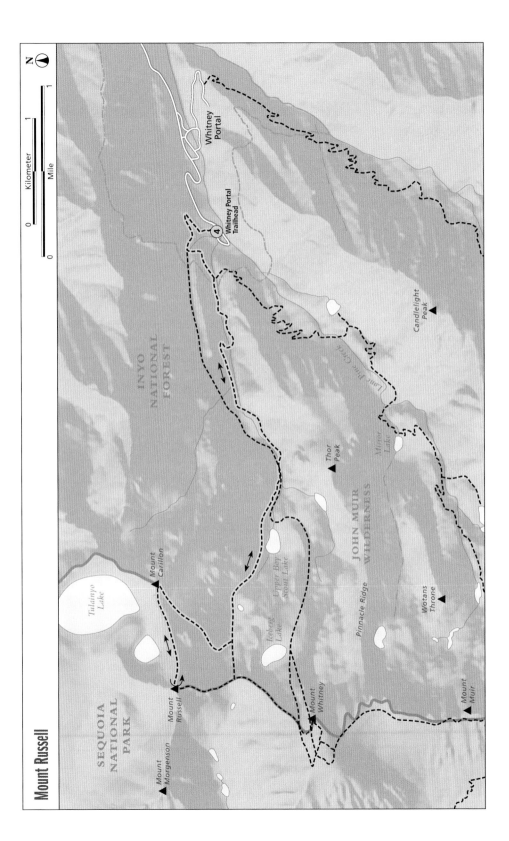

SEQUOIA NATIONAL PARK

INYO NATIONAL FOREST

JOHN MUIR WILDERNESS

Tulainyo Lake

Mount Morgenson ▲

Mount Russell ▲

Mount Carillon ▲

Iceberg Lake

Upper Boy Scout Lake

Mount Whitney ▲

Pinnacle Ridge

Thor Peak ▲

Lone Pine Creek

Mirror Lake

Mount Muir ▲

Wotans Throne ▲

Candlelight Peak ▲

Whitney Portal

Whitney Portal Trailhead

④

N

0   1
Kilometer
0   1
Mile

commonly occur when the trail is clear, the consequences are far greater when snow and ice are present.

Without adequate training and skills with both crampons and ice axe, you will endanger not only yourself but those around you as well. The physical exertion of climbing combined with the unpredictable footing that ice and snow provide can lead to slips and falls. Falls of this nature can go for hundreds of feet, resulting in injury, rescue, and, in extreme cases, death. Be mindful of your party's skill set if you encounter frozen conditions. The mountains will always be there, and you can always try again if the danger level seems high. Stories about your hike will be best told by you. Be smart and get back home safely.

Leaving Trail Camp you will immediately start the ascent of the infamous switch-backs to Trail Crest. From this vista there are just a couple of miles to the top of Mount Whitney. Once you have reached the highest point in the lower 48 states, Mount Russell lies to the north.

Descend the Mountaineer's Route trail lying north of the Smithsonian Hut. Use the ledges on both sides of the gully to reach the notch that marks the top of the couloir used to climb up from Ice Berg Lake. At this point Mount Russell will be visible to the northeast. Downclimb the couloir using the ledges on either side.

During winter and early season, snow and ice may be encountered and ice axes and crampons will be required to safely climb down. Always check on the current trail conditions and the pending weather forecast before leaving the trailhead. If you do not possess the skills and knowledge to use snow and ice tools, *do not* attempt to pass through these sections.

Once the bottom of the couloir has been reached, follow the unmaintained trail to the lower end of Upper Boy Scout Lake. Route-finding to Upper Boy Scout Lake can become challenging. You will encounter several trail options. Take the trail found just above the willow trees. You may encounter route cairns that will help guide you through the talus and rocky slabs that lie between the two lakes. The distance from the trailhead to Upper Boy Scout Lake will be just a shade over 3.5 miles. Avoid bushwhacking through the willow trees and undergrowth. If you are planning on making this a multiday trip, set up camp here. This location also makes a great approach point to Mount Russell.

Above (north/northwest), you will see a scree and sand hill. The Class 2 climbing up the scree can be a slippery challenge, as the surface can slip underfoot. You will be able to follow in the footsteps of climbers who have come before on the scree sections. The sand will slow your progress down, but eventually the saddle between Russell and Carillon will be reached. Do not get discouraged by the one-step-forward-two-steps-back mental grind of this section. Frustration just becomes wasted energy.

Once you gain the saddle, Mount Russell stands right in front of you. Walk the short distance to the start of the east ridge where the route is worn and defined. Scramble over the first little bit; there will be some exposure but the moves are pretty straightforward. The route follows the north side of the ridge for much of the remaining climb. If you are climbing in the early season when snow and ice are present, hiking up the crest, even with its greater level of exposure, will be the safer route. North of the ridge you will encounter a gully just before the lower east summit. Continue along the crest and past a small saddle.

To reach the true summit from this point, you will have to traverse a series of ledges on the north side of the ridge. When you are directly below the summit block, climb the blocks and ledges to the peak. This Class 3 section does have some exposure, but the moves are not too difficult. The summit block provides an amazing view of Mount Whitney and Mount Muir to the south and on a clear day Mount Williamson to the north. The Alabama Hills and Lone Pine will be off to the east in the valley below.

Descend by carefully retracing your steps back to Upper Boy Scout Lake. Keep just above the willow trees and undergrowth along the unmaintained trail and navigate through the Ebersbacher Ledges to reach the North Fork Lone Pine Creek. Follow the trail until it joins the Whitney Portal Trail. Just a few minutes farther down the trail, and you will reach the parking lot.

Hiking Information

Closest Outfitters

Big Willi Mountaineering Company, 120 S. Main St., Ste. 13 and 14, Lone Pine, CA 93545; (760) 878-2849; https://bigwillimc.com

Stop in for last-minute supplies and ask Blair about his favorite places to explore in the Sierras. If you are driving north on US 395 from picking up your permit, Big Willi is located just past the stoplight in Lone Pine.

Whitney Portal Store, Whitney Portal Trailhead; (760) 876-0030; www.whitney portalstore.com

Great Pre- or Post-Mountain Spots

Whitney Portal Store, Whitney Portal Trailhead; (760) 876-0030; www.whitney portalstore.com

From its trailside location, the Whitney Portal Store serves up huge pancakes to fuel your climb, made-to-order burgers to reward success, cold beer to wash it all down with, and the most up-to-date trail and mountain conditions available. This family-owned store has been taking care of hiker needs for decades and offers live webcam views of Mount Whitney.

Mt. Whitney Restaurant, 227 S. Main St., Lone Pine, CA 93545; (760) 876-5751

Great place to fuel up before heading to any of the trailheads in the area. Over the years, Hollywood's stars have dined here while filming in the Alabama Hills.

Shuttle Service

Eastern Sierra Shuttle Service, Lone Pine, CA; info@mountwhitneyshuttle .com

From well below her summit, Mount Whitney looms as a granite giant over the region. As you pass through the Alabama Hills and up the road to the Whitney Portal Trail, the mountain comes into view to take your breath away.

5 Mount Williamson

Elevation: 14,375 feet, 2nd highest
Start: Shepards Pass Hiker Trailhead
Distance: 28 miles round-trip
Primary route: Shepards Pass to West Chute
Elevation gain: 6,657 feet
Hiking time: 12 to 18 hours
Difficulty: Class 1, Class 3
Trail surface: Dirt trail leading to talus, exposed scramble
Trailhead elevation: 6,300 feet
Camping: Dispersed camping at trailhead, designated sites at Mahogany Flat and Anvil Camp, dispersed camping above Shepards Pass
Fees: None

Permit: Yes
Best seasons: Summer and fall; technical winter climb
Maps: Tom Harrison Mt. Whitney High Country; Wilderness Press Mt. Whitney; USGS Mount Williamson
Nearest town: Independence, CA
Trail contact: Mount Whitney Ranger District, PO Box 8, Lone Pine, CA 93545; (760) 876-6200
First ascent: July 10, 1903, Joseph LeConte, R. Butler, E. Gould, T. Parker, A. Elston, and A. Eells

Finding the trailhead: From Independence, at the intersection of US 395 and Market Street, go west toward the mountains on Market Street, which becomes Onion Valley Road. At 4.5 miles, turn left (south) onto Foothill Road. At 7.5 miles, bear left at the fork in the road, following the sign for the Shepards Pass Hiker Trail. In 8.4 miles, turn right (toward the mountains). At 9.2 miles, arrive at the Shepards Pass Trailhead. GPS: 36.65610°N / 118.3103°W

The Hike

The relative proximity of Mount Williamson and Mount Tyndall to each other coupled with the shared access from Shepards Pass makes these two mountains easier to climb as a pair than individually. Separated by less than 2 miles and the Williamson Bowl, bagging both of them on the same trip saves time and unnecessary elevation gain/loss over making two trips. While each summit can be reached on its own, combining the approach to these two as a pair makes for a solid weekend of climbing. A combination summit attempt means only one hike up to Shepards Pass from the trailhead will be necessary.

The drive to the trailhead is pretty straightforward. While it is always advisable to travel on the NFS access roads with a high-clearance vehicle, it is possible to reach the parking area in a standard car. As you drive along Foothill Road, Mount Williamson will peek into view. The second tallest of the California fourteeners is also visible from US 395 on the way into Independence. The parking area is relatively large and marked with an informational sign.

It is very possible to summit both mountains in a day. The total distance would be under 30 miles, and with a predawn start, a fit and capable individual could be back at the trailhead in under a day. Most people, planning on at least two days, will hike up

Mount Williamson will be visible from US 395 and the drive to the trailhead on Foothill Road, but the view from the Hiker Trail on the way to Shepards Pass in late spring can take your breath away.

With Mount Williamson in the distance, the approach up Shepards Pass provides the opportunity to pitch your tent and enjoy the tranquility of the backcountry.

to either Mahogany Flat or Anvil Camp on the east side of Shepards Pass and camp, or they will crest the pass and set their tents near Tyndall Creek or in the Williamson Bowl. Since the trail reaches Shepards Pass from the east and the sun sets in the west (and on the far side of the pass), darkness will arrive about an hour earlier than one would expect, so keep this in mind when you depart the parking area.

Trail conditions will vary greatly depending on the time of year you are climbing. During the winter and into late spring, you will likely encounter snow as low as Mahogany Flat and all the way to Shepards Pass and beyond. These conditions will require crampons or micro-spikes and an ice axe for safety. As the snow melts, the water level in Symmes Creek and Shepards Creek can become dangerously high. At various points the trail will traverse scree fields, making footing loose and slick during the early climbing period. Due to the steepness of the drainage that is home to Shepards Creek, down-mountain winds can blow hard and fast.

Water sources are abundant throughout the entire hike. In addition to Symmes Creek, the trail crosses several natural springs. At both Mahogany Flat and Anvil Camp, Shepards Creek is accessible. Water can also be found around the "Pothole." Once you crest Shepards Pass, Tyndall Creek and several tarns serve as water sources. Having so many water sources means that you can eliminate some weight in your pack by filling your bottle often. Remember that water will be the single heaviest item in your pack, but keep in mind that you need to stay hydrated to perform at your physical and mental best.

In the 10.5 miles from the trailhead to Shepards Pass, almost 8,000 feet of vertical await you. The trail climbs away from the Owens Valley and, just a few minutes later, crosses Symmes Creek for the first time. In the springtime the snowmelt water may reach knee height. While the water will be cold, the creek bottom is relatively smooth, so you could make this crossing barefoot. Otherwise, it is advisable to pack dry socks and footwear to prevent chafing and blisters later in the hike. During the summer months the creek can be crossed with ease and without submerging your feet. Depending on water levels, you will cross Symmes Creek two or three times within the first hour of hiking. Foot care is vital to a successful and enjoyable backcountry trip, so make sure that your feet are as dry as possible after crossing the creek.

Leaving Symmes Creek behind, the trail switchbacks its way toward Mahogany Flat, and in about 4 miles, Mount Williamson comes into view as you crest an unnamed pass. There are several protected campsites to the left of the trail. The trail drops away from the pass and crosses some scree fields and a small stream before climbing up to Mahogany Flat a mile or so later. At just under halfway to the pass, this is a popular place to camp. A trail leads down to the creek below to refill water if needed. In late May and early June, do not be surprised to find patches of snow as you begin to switchback up the trail below Mount Keith to the north. While the trail conditions may vary, the overall footing will be solid and without exposure.

Anvil Camp, right at the tree line, will be your next landmark. If you camp here, be mindful of the mosquitoes and blackflies during the warmer months. Above Anvil Camp, the boulder and talus fields of the Pothole begin. Late in the season, the trail will be clearly defined and easy to follow. In the spring, however, the conditions can be more challenging. Due to the sun protection created by the ridge to the south and the pass above, the final mile in distance and 1,000 feet in elevation gain up to Shepards Pass can be choked with snow during this period.

Keep an eye out for the clouds that can form on the other side of the pass. Clear and bright days can rapidly become dark and stormy at 11,000 feet. While there is minimal shelter and protection here, it will be infinitely safer to camp below the pass than to get caught in a thunderstorm or blizzard on top. Due to the steep elevation changes from the trailhead to the pass, down-mountain winds can reach gale-force

Looking toward Shepards Pass to the east, the base of Mount Tyndall's north ridge approach awaits.

level. Since we will have gained almost 5,000 feet in elevation, the air temperature will have decreased dramatically as well.

To successfully and safely reach the pass via a snow-covered trail, you will need to break out your ice axe and crampons. With parts of the trail covered with snow, traversing the talus field will be easier than hopping from rock to rock. Bear in mind that the trail, without snow cover, is very well defined and easy to follow all the way to the top of the pass. The trail will follow a series of switchbacks up the right side of the face, but when there are frozen conditions, those ice tools come in handy. Instead of hiking back and forth across the face on a dry trail, use your crampons to kick steps and move vertically up the final pitch to the top. Unless you are extremely comfortable with using an ice axe and wearing crampons, do not attempt to climb Shepards Pass under these conditions. You will put yourself, and those you are climbing with, at risk for injury or worse.

Cresting the top of the pass, Mount Tyndall comes into view for the first time directly ahead of you as the corner is rounded. Up-and-back day hikers will proceed to either the northwest slope of Mount Tyndall or into the Williamson Bowl to approach Mount Williamson.

Always be aware of how rapidly weather conditions can change in the mountains. Checking the forecast before heading up the trail is a must, but conditions can deteriorate in a matter of seconds in the Sierras. On this late May trip, the forecast called for blue skies, low wind, and no snow. As we approached the Pothole below Shepards Pass, the weather flipped as the wind came up and the skies clouded over, forcing us to dig in for the night. With wind chills in the single digits and almost a foot of snow falling, the three-season-rated Big Agnes tents and my Western Mountaineering Kodiak sleeping bag kept me warm and toasty all through the night. Summit fever is a very real thing, but sometimes you have to pay attention to the messages Mother Nature sends. We chose to safely return to the trailhead. The mountains will always be there, but you have to be alive to climb them.

To make an approach to Mount Williamson from the top of Shepards Pass, head southeast to cross the saddle northwest of Mount Tyndall. This will lead you into the talus-filled Williamson Bowl. This seemingly endless field of boulders must be crossed to reach the summit. For many this section will be the most mentally trying challenge in reaching the top of the mountain. Timing your trip to coincide with some snow cover can make the tedium of crossing Williamson Bowl far less.

When the snow cover has melted, several lakes will be visible as you enter the bowl heading toward the second lake. Use the first lake at the base of Mount Tyndall (west of the route) as the first reference point to start the traverse of Williamson Bowl. Rounding the second lake, the West Chute route will be visible to the east as you continue to move through the talus. The route looks like an S from below as it snakes from the right to left and then back right up the mountain.

On the west face of Mount Williamson, you can see a rock band with dark black water marks. The route climbs toward the darkest and most prominent water mark. At this point, continue up the talus to the right of the mark to the large chute. Enter the chute and continue up for about 1,000 feet. Stay in the main chute and avoid taking branches that dead-end or increase your exposure. At the top of the chute, your direct route is blocked by a rocky cliff. Traverse right (southeast) for 20 to 30 feet and enter a short Class 3 chimney for the final pitch to the summit. The hand- and footholds are easy to grasp and the chimney is easily maneuvered through.

Emerging from the chimney, you will step out onto the summit plateau and a short walk to what is considered the true summit of Mount Williamson to the south. Three points on Mount Williamson are taller than 14,000 feet. The "South Summit" stands the tallest and is where the summit register box is located. The Owens Valley will stretch out to your east and, on a clear day, Mount Whitney can be seen to the south. Downclimb the chimney and follow your steps back down to the bowl. Traverse back toward Shepards Pass to either reach the north slope approach to Mount Tyndall or return to the trailhead.

Extended Route: Whitney Portal Trail to Shepards Pass

Finding the trailhead: From Lone Pine, at the intersection of US 395 and Whitney Portal Road, head west (toward the mountains). In 13 miles, arrive at the Whitney Portal Trailhead parking area. GPS: 36.57860°N / 118.293°W

This multiday route starts at the Whitney Portal Trailhead and will require an overnight permit. Since this hike finishes at the Shepards Pass Trailhead, you will need to either arrange for shuttle service or other transportation or hike back to your car. Since this route passes near the approaches to both Mount Muir and Mount Whitney, the ability to summit three fourteeners in one trip is very possible. Peak baggers can also add Mount Tyndall to the trip to add a fourth summit.

Begin hiking up the trail just steps from the Whitney Portal Store. Depending on the season and time of day, expect to encounter up to 100 people a day on the way to Trail Crest. There are two designated camping locations along the eastern approach.

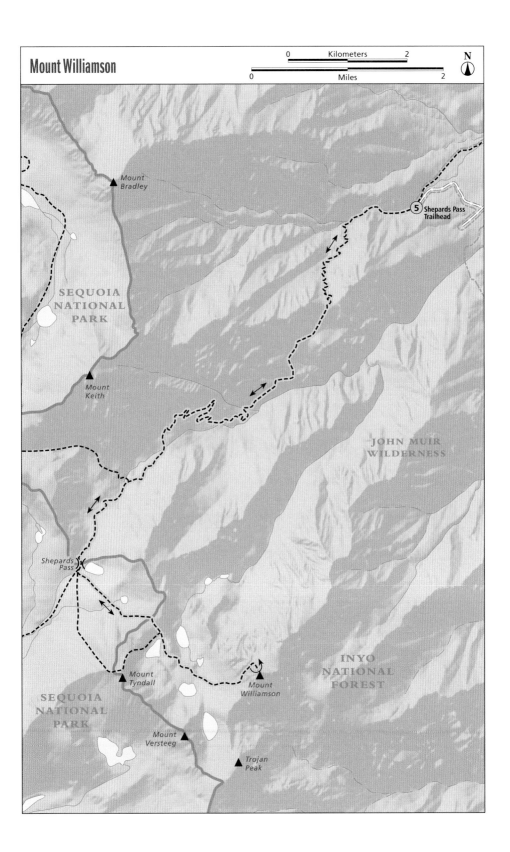

Mount Williamson

Kilometers

Miles

N

Mount Bradley

SEQUOIA NATIONAL PARK

Mount Keith

5 Shepards Pass Trailhead

JOHN MUIR WILDERNESS

Shepards Pass

INYO NATIONAL FOREST

Mount Tyndall

Mount Williamson

SEQUOIA NATIONAL PARK

Mount Versteeg

Trojan Peak

Outpost Camp and Trail Camp are the only locations where pitching a tent is allowed on the way up the trail.

Reaching these locations will take several hours for most people, and the luxury of stretching out and relaxing before the final summit push will be welcome. Situated above the tree line, Trail Camp does not offer much in the way of protection from the sun, so choose your spot wisely. The camp lies just below the start of Whitney's infamous 99 switchbacks, so you can get a look at the 2 miles of granite trail waiting for you.

For a variety of reasons, it is smart to get an early start on your summit push. Once you start the next section of the hike, there will not be any consistent protection from the sun that beats down on the trail. Leaving at a predawn hour will eliminate most of the blazing sun on the way up. Since the trail traffic is regulated by permits, starting early will also help avoid getting caught behind slower groups on the trail. Thunderstorms can arrive without much advance warning in the afternoon. Getting caught on an exposed ridge in a lightning storm will potentially result in serious injury, so plan to be down before afternoon if possible.

Mentally, there is an advantage to leaving in the dark. The actual hiking distance from Trail Camp to Trail Crest on the switchbacks is 2.2 miles. The direct distance is about half of that, which means that in roughly 1 mile the elevation changes 1,140 feet. The switchbacks meander up the cliff face at a pitch that most can hike with relative ease. Traversing back and forth every few minutes, the pass at Trail Crest pops in and out of view. It becomes easy to look too far ahead and feel like the progress being made is not much progress at all. Leaving Trail Camp while it is still dark eliminates the ability to look too far up the trail. You can only focus on the trail that your headlamp illuminates right in front of you. Looking up, Trail Crest will not be visible. Looking down will reveal the headlamps of other climbers on the trail behind you. This section can be a bottleneck, as the travel pace will be relatively slow.

In the spring, early summer, and late fall, you may encounter snow and ice covering the trail above the tree line. Travel from Trail Camp to Trail Crest will not utilize the famous switchbacks; rather, you will use your crampons and ice axe to traverse the chute. An understanding of how these pieces of equipment should be used is necessary before showing up at the trailhead. Make sure your ice axe has a leash so that it does not slide away from you if it falls. Always keep your axe in your uphill hand. Practice self-arrest techniques with the ice axe so that you can react quickly should you start to slide down the mountain. Your ice axe can save you from injury or worse. Crampons provide an additional level of traction while walking on frozen surfaces. Please seek instruction from a trained professional on how to use these ice tools.

If you do not possess the skills to competently use an ice axe and crampons, *do not* attempt to climb the chute to Trail Crest. You should call ahead for current weather conditions to be prepared. Due to the lottery system for Mount Whitney permits, many people approach the mountain without taking the trail conditions into consideration, feeling that since they "won" a permit, they have to attempt the climb. Summit fever can be a dangerous thing. While dehydration and altitude sickness commonly occur when the trail is clear, the consequences are far greater when snow and ice are present.

Once Trail Crest has been gained, look for the intersection of the John Muir Trail (JMT) coming up from the valley floor to the west. It will only take a few moments of hiking to find the trail. It is important to note that the approaches to both Mount Muir and Mount Whitney are within 2 miles of the junction.

With Hitchcock Lakes shimmering below you to the southwest, start down the JMT switchbacks. The route will be well defined and easy to follow as you descend to the valley floor. Fresh water will be abundant through streams and lakes once the valley is reached. There will be under 7 miles of distance and 3,000 feet of elevation loss from the ridgeline to the junction of the JMT and the Pacific Crest Trail (PCT).

Turn right (north) at this intersection. You will find that the trail maintains an average elevation right around 10,000 feet for almost 8 miles. Use the intersection of the High Sierra Trail, coming from the west, 3.4 miles up the PCT/JMT as a landmark. Wallace Creek will also be crossed at this point. For purists and historians, the approach to Mount Barnard will present itself a few minutes later.

Continue on the PCT/JMT for an additional 4.2 miles. You will see signs for the Tyndall Creek ranger cabin. At this point look for the trail to Shepards Pass heading to the northeast. A gradual 2,000 feet of elevation gain over 3.5 miles brings the north side of Williamson Bowl into view.

To make an approach to Mount Williamson from the top of Shepards Pass, head southeast to cross the saddle northwest of Mount Tyndall. This will lead you into the talus-filled Williamson Bowl. This seemingly endless field of boulders must be crossed to reach the summit. For many this section will be the most mentally trying challenge in reaching the top of the mountain. Timing your trip to coincide with some snow cover can make the tedium of crossing Williamson Bowl far less.

When the snow cover has melted, several lakes will be visible as you enter the bowl heading toward the second lake. Use the first lake at the base of Mount Tyndall (west of the route) as the first reference point to start the traverse of Williamson Bowl. Rounding the second lake, the West Chute route will be visible to the east as you continue to move through the talus. The route looks like an S from below as it snakes from the right to left and then back right up the mountain.

On the west face of Mount Williamson, you can see a rock band with dark black water marks. The route climbs toward the darkest and most prominent water mark. At this point, continue up the talus to the right of the mark to the large chute. Enter the chute and continue up for about 1,000 feet. Stay in the main chute and avoid taking branches that dead-end or increase your exposure. At the top of the chute, your direct route is blocked by a rocky cliff. Traverse right (southeast) for 20 to 30 feet and enter a short Class 3 chimney for the final pitch to the summit. The hand- and footholds are easy to grasp and the chimney is easily maneuvered through.

Emerging from the chimney, you will step out onto the summit plateau and a short walk to what is considered the true summit of Mount Williamson to the south. Three points on Mount Williamson are taller than 14,000 feet. The "South Summit" stands the tallest and is where the summit register box is located. The Owens Valley will stretch out to your east and, on a clear day, Mount Whitney can be seen to the south. Downclimb the chimney and follow your steps back down to the bowl. Traverse back toward Shepards Pass to either reach the north slope approach to Mount Tyndall or return to the trailhead.

The return hike from Shepards Pass may require you to cross some snow or ice as you start down. Expect to encounter at least a few stretches of frozen ground even late into the season. The use of micro-spikes would be smart. Be mindful of foot placement, as the fall could be catastrophic. In winter and early season, make sure to have crampons and an ice axe for safety.

There will be flowing fresh water along the trail for most of the descent. Anvil Camp is a great place to stop and catch your breath but be mindful that the mosquitoes are thick during warmer weather. The remaining miles feature views of Mount Williamson and the Owens Valley.

Hiking Information

Closest Outfitters

Big Willi Mountaineering Company, 120 S. Main St., Ste. 13 and 14, Lone Pine, CA 93545; (760) 878-2849; https://bigwillimc.com

Stop in for last-minute supplies and ask Blair about his favorite places to explore in the Sierras. If you are driving north on US 395 from picking up your permit, Big Willi is located just past the stoplight in Lone Pine.

Carroll's Market, 136 S. Main St., Big Pine, CA 93513

Great Pre- or Post-Mountain Spots

Copper Top BBQ, 310 S. Main St., Big Pine, CA 93513; (760) 970-5577; www .coppertopbbq.com

Voted the "Best Barbeque" in the country in 2015, this roadside take-out stand has become a food destination for folks across the country. Huge fan of the tri-tip after a few days in the mountains.

Aberdeen Restaurant, 150 Tinemaha Rd., Independence, CA 93526; (760) 938-2663; www.aberdeenresort.com

Shuttle Service

East Side Shuttle Service, Independence, CA; (760) 878-8047; paul@inyopro .com; www.eastsidesierrashuttle.com

6 Mount Tyndall

Elevation: 14,018 feet, 12th highest	**Fees:** None
Start: Shepards Pass Hiker Trailhead	**Permit:** Yes
Distance: 26 miles round-trip	**Best seasons:** Summer and fall; technical
Primary route: Shepards Pass to Northwest	winter climb
Ridge	**Maps:** Tom Harrison Mt. Whitney High Country;
Elevation gain: 7,718 feet	Wilderness Press Mt. Whitney; USGS Mount
Hiking time: 12 to 18 hours	Williamson
Difficulty: Class 1, Class 2/3	**Nearest town:** Independence, CA
Trail surface: Dirt trail leading to talus,	**Trail contact:** Mount Whitney Ranger Dis-
medium-exposure scramble	trict, PO Box 8, Lone Pine, CA 93545; (760)
Trailhead elevation: 6,300 feet	876-6200
Camping: Dispersed camping at trailhead, des-	**First ascent:** July 6, 1864, Clarence King and
ignated sites at Mahogany Flat and Anvil Camp,	Richard Cotter
dispersed camping above Shepards Pass	

Finding the trailhead: From Independence, at the intersection of US 395 and Market Street, go west toward the mountains on Market Street, which becomes Onion Valley Road. At 4.5 miles, turn left (south) onto Foothill Road. At 7.5 miles, bear left at the fork in the road, following the sign for the Shepards Pass Hiker Trail. In 8.4 miles, turn right (toward the mountains). At 9.2 miles, arrive at the Shepards Pass Trailhead. GPS: 36.65610°N / 118.3103°W

The Hike

It is very possible to summit Mount Williamson and Mount Tyndall in a day. The total distance would be under 30 miles, and with a predawn start, a fit and capable individual could be back at the trailhead in under a day. Since the two mountains lie within a short distance of each other and the hike up Shepards Pass will have already been completed, plan on camping in the Williamson Bowl and tagging both summits. Most people, planning on at least two days, will hike up to either Mahogany Flat or Anvil Camp on the east side of Shepards Pass and camp, or they will crest the pass and set their tents near Tyndall Creek or in Williamson Bowl. Since the trail reaches Shepards Pass from the east and the sun sets in the west (and on the far side of the pass), darkness will arrive about an hour earlier than one would expect, so keep this in mind when you depart the parking area.

Trail conditions will vary greatly depending on the time of year you are climbing. During the winter and into late spring, you will likely encounter snow as low as Mahogany Flat and all the way to Shepards Pass and beyond. These conditions will require crampons or micro-spikes and an ice axe for safety. As the snow melts, the water level in Symmes Creek and Shepards Creek can become dangerously high. At various points the trail will traverse scree fields, making footing loose and slick during the early climbing period. Due to the steepness of the drainage that is home to Shepards Creek, down-mountain winds can blow hard and fast.

Water sources are abundant throughout the entire hike. In addition to Symmes Creek, the trail crosses several natural springs. At both Mahogany Flat and Anvil Camp, Shepards Creek is accessible. Water can also be found around the "Pothole." Once you crest Shepards Pass, Tyndall Creek and several tarns serve as water sources. Having so many water sources means that you can eliminate some weight in your pack by filling your bottle often. Remember that water will be the single heaviest item in your pack, but keep in mind that you need to stay hydrated to perform at your physical and mental best.

In the 10.5 miles from the trailhead to Shepards Pass, almost 8,000 feet of vertical await you. The trail climbs away from the Owens Valley and, just a few minutes later, crosses Symmes Creek for the first time. In the springtime the snowmelt water may reach knee height. While the water will be cold, the creek bottom is relatively smooth, so you could make this crossing barefoot. Otherwise, it is advisable to pack dry socks and footwear to prevent chafing and blisters later in the hike. During the summer months, the creek can be crossed with ease and without submerging your feet. Depending on water levels, you will cross Symmes Creek two or three times within the first hour of hiking. Foot care is vital to a successful and enjoyable backcountry trip, so make sure that your feet are as dry as possible after crossing the creek.

Leaving Symmes Creek behind, the trail switchbacks its way toward Mahogany Flat and in about 4 miles, Mount Williamson comes into view as you crest an unnamed pass. There are several protected campsites to the left of the trail. The trail drops away from the pass and crosses some scree fields and a small stream before climbing up to Mahogany Flat a mile or so later. At just under halfway to the pass, this is a popular place to camp. A trail leads down to the creek below to refill water

During a late spring trip, Karina Redding leads the way toward Shepards Pass.

Mount Williamson will be visible from US 395 and the drive to the trailhead on Foothill Road, but the view from the Hiker Trail on the way to Shepards Pass in late spring can take your breath away.

if needed. In late May and early June, do not be surprised to find patches of snow as you begin to switchback up the trail below Mount Keith to the north. While the trail conditions may vary, the overall footing will be solid and without exposure.

Anvil Camp, right at the tree line, will be your next landmark. If you camp here, be mindful of the mosquitoes and blackflies during the warmer months. Above Anvil Camp, the boulder and talus fields of the Pothole begin. Late in the season, the trail will be clearly defined and easy to follow. In the spring, however, the conditions can be more challenging. Due to the sun protection created by the ridge to the south and the pass above, the final mile in distance and 1,000 feet in elevation gain up to Shepards Pass can be choked with snow during this period.

Keep an eye out for the clouds that can form on the other side of the pass. Clear and bright days can rapidly become dark and stormy at 11,000 feet. While there is minimal shelter and protection here, it will be infinitely safer to camp below the pass than to get caught in a thunderstorm or blizzard on top. Due to the steep elevation changes from the trailhead to the pass, down-mountain winds can reach gale-force level. Since we will have gained almost 5,000 feet in elevation, the air temperature will have decreased dramatically as well.

To successfully and safely reach the pass via a snow-covered trail, you will need to break out your ice axe and crampons. With parts of the trail covered with snow, traversing the talus field will be easier than hopping from rock to rock. Bear in mind that the trail, without snow cover, is very well defined and easy to follow all the way to the top of the pass. The trail will follow a series of switchbacks up the right side of the face, but when there are frozen conditions, those ice tools come in handy. Instead

Mount Tyndall

of hiking back and forth across the face on a dry trail, use your crampons to kick steps and move vertically up the final pitch to the top. Unless you are extremely comfortable with using an ice axe and wearing crampons, do not attempt to climb Shepards Pass under these conditions. You will put yourself, and those you are climbing with, at risk for injury or worse.

Cresting the top of the pass, Mount Tyndall comes into view for the first time directly ahead of you as the corner is rounded. Up-and-back day hikers will proceed to either the northwest slope of Mount Tyndall or into Williamson Bowl to approach Mount Williamson.

Assuming that your climb will be during the warm and dry months, you will not need your crampons or ice axe to bag this summit. Be smart and give yourself plenty of daylight time to work with, as the final summit route can be intimidating in the waning hours of the day.

Continuing on the Shepards Pass Hiker Trail, the approach to Mount Tyndall will begin about a half mile down the trail. At this point you will be close to the start of

Christie Christianson looks down on the Owens Valley from the trail to Shepards Pass.

Once you crest Shepards Pass, Mount Tyndall will rise before you. Make your way to the base of the northwest ridge and hike to the summit on the Class 2 route in dry months. During early and late season, crampons will be required.

the ridgeline at about 11,800 feet. Climbing up the right (west) side of the ridge, the trail will be rocky and loose at times. There are some rock slabs that can be utilized in traversing this section if preferred. To reach the summit ridge, work around the west side of the prominent gendarme just beyond a trail intersection. There is some exposure here, which at first blush looks far more daunting than it is in reality. Maintain a position on the west side of the ridge until you reach the summit. Reaching the summit via this Class 2 route is by far the easiest and safest. Return to the valley below simply by retracing your steps.

Add the snow and ice of a winter or spring climb, and the inherent risks increase. Chances are you will still be wearing your crampons and holding your ice axe after reaching the top of Shepards Pass. You will find that some sections of the ridge will be snow- or ice-covered and some areas will be free and clear. Move slowly with calculated deliberation across frozen sections. As with the approach to Shepards Pass, snow cover can eliminate the tedious process of stepping from boulder to boulder, making straight-line travel possible. The dangers lie in the quality of the surface. Snow can fall away, causing avalanches. Kick steps into the surface to ensure a solid base to put weight on. Keep your ice axe in your uphill hand in case you slip and need to self-arrest. On your way back down the trail, keep your weight over your center of mass to maintain balance.

Heading back to Shepards Pass and to the trailhead will take you right down the same trail.

Extended Route: Whitney Portal Trail to Shepards Pass

Finding the trailhead: From Lone Pine, at the intersection of US 395 and Whitney Portal Road, head west (toward the mountains). In 13 miles, arrive at the Whitney Portal Trailhead parking area. GPS: 36.57860°N / 118.293°W

This multiday route starts at the Whitney Portal Trailhead and will require an overnight permit. Since this hike finishes at the Shepards Pass Trailhead, you will need to either arrange for shuttle service or other transportation or hike back to your car. Since this route passes near the approaches to both Mount Muir and Mount Whitney, the ability to summit three fourteeners in one trip is very viable. With Mount Williamson in such close proximity, consider adding this fourth summit to the trip.

Begin hiking up the trail just steps from the Whitney Portal Store. Depending on the season and time of day, expect to encounter up to 100 people a day on the way to Trail Crest. There are two designated camping locations along the eastern approach. Outpost Camp and Trail Camp are the only locations where pitching a tent is allowed on the way up the trail.

Reaching these locations will take several hours for most people, and the luxury of stretching out and relaxing before the final summit push will be welcome. Situated above the tree line, Trail Camp does not offer much in the way of protection from the sun, so choose your spot wisely. The camp lies just below the start of Whitney's infamous 99 switchbacks, so you can get a look at the 2 miles of granite trail waiting for you.

For a variety of reasons, it is smart to get an early start on your summit push. Once you start the next section of the hike, there will not be any consistent protection from the sun that beats down on the trail. Leaving at a predawn hour will eliminate most of the blazing sun on the way up. Since the trail traffic is regulated by permits, starting early will also help avoid getting caught behind slower groups on the trail. Thunderstorms can arrive without much advance warning in the afternoon. Getting caught on an exposed ridge in a lightning storm will potentially result in serious injury, so plan to be down before afternoon.

Mentally, there is an advantage to leaving in the dark. The actual hiking distance from Trail Camp to Trail Crest on the switchbacks is 2.2 miles. The direct distance is about half of that, which means that in roughly 1 mile the elevation changes 1,140 feet. The switchbacks meander up the cliff face at a pitch that most can hike with relative ease. Traversing back and forth every few minutes, the pass at Trail Crest pops in and out of view. It becomes easy to look too far ahead and feel like the progress being made is not much progress at all. Leaving Trail Camp while it is still dark eliminates the ability to look too far up the trail. You can only focus on the trail that your

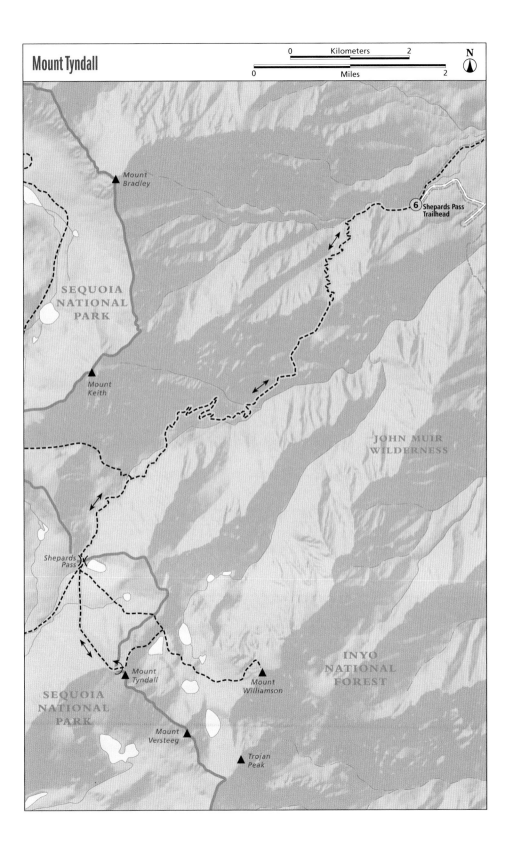

Mount Tyndall

Kilometers
0 2

Miles
0 2

N

Mount
Bradley

6 Shepards Pass
Trailhead

SEQUOIA
NATIONAL
PARK

Mount
Keith

JOHN MUIR
WILDERNESS

Shepards
Pass

INYO
NATIONAL
FOREST

Mount Tyndall

Mount
Williamson

SEQUOIA
NATIONAL
PARK

Mount
Versteeg

Trojan
Peak

headlamp illuminates right in front of you. Looking up, Trail Crest will not be visible. Looking down will reveal the headlamps of other climbers on the trail behind you. This section can be a bottleneck, as the travel pace will be relatively slow.

In the spring, early summer, and late fall, you may encounter snow and ice covering the trail above the tree line. Travel from Trail Camp to Trail Crest will not utilize the famous switchbacks; rather, you will use your crampons and ice axe to traverse the chute. An understanding of how these pieces of equipment should be used is necessary before showing up at the trailhead. Make sure your ice axe has a leash so that it does not slide away from you if it falls. Always keep your axe in your uphill hand. Practice self-arrest techniques with the ice axe so that you can react quickly should you start to slide down the mountain. Your ice axe can save you from injury or worse. Crampons provide an additional level of traction while walking on frozen surfaces. Please seek instruction from a trained professional on how to use these ice tools.

If you do not possess the skills to competently use an ice axe and crampons, *do not* attempt to climb the chute to Trail Crest. You should call ahead for current weather conditions to be prepared. Due to the lottery system for Mount Whitney permits, many people approach the mountain without taking the trail conditions into consideration, feeling that since they "won" a permit, they have to attempt the climb. Summit fever can be a dangerous thing. While dehydration and altitude sickness commonly occur when the trail is clear, the consequences are far greater when snow and ice are present.

Once Trail Crest has been gained, look for the intersection of the John Muir Trail (JMT) coming up from the valley floor to the west. It will only take a few moments of hiking to find the trail. It is important to note that the approaches to both Mount Muir and Mount Whitney are within 2 miles of the junction.

With Hitchcock Lakes shimmering below you to the southwest, start down the JMT switchbacks. The route will be well defined and easy to follow as you descend to the valley floor. Fresh water will be abundant through streams and lakes once the valley is reached. There will be under 7 miles of distance and 3,000 feet of elevation loss from the ridgeline to the junction of the JMT and the Pacific Crest Trail (PCT).

Turn right (north) at this intersection. You will find that the trail maintains an average elevation right around 10,000 feet for almost 8 miles. Use the intersection of the High Sierra Trail, coming from the west, 3.4 miles up the PCT/JMT as a landmark. Wallace Creek will also be crossed at this point. For purists and historians, the approach to Mount Barnard will present itself a few minutes later.

Continue on the PCT/JMT for an additional 4.2 miles. You will see signs for the Tyndall Creek ranger cabin. At this point look for the trail to Shepards Pass heading to the northeast. A gradual 2,000 feet of elevation gain over 3.5 miles brings the approach to Mount Tyndall into view.

The Class 2 approach to Mount Tyndall will begin about a half mile down off the trail to the south. Shoot for the low trail and follow the cairns to start the climb. At this point you will be close to the start of the ridgeline at about 11,800 feet. Climbing up the right (west) side of the ridge, the trail will be rocky and loose at times. There are some rock slabs that can be utilized in traversing this section if preferred. To reach the summit ridge, work around the west side of the prominent gendarme just beyond a trail intersection. There is some exposure here, which at first blush looks far more daunting than it is in reality. Maintain a position on the west side of the ridge until you reach the summit. Reaching the summit via this Class 2 route is by far the easiest and safest. Return to the valley below simply by retracing your steps.

Add the snow and ice of a winter or spring climb, and the inherent risks increase. Chances are you will still be wearing your crampons and holding your ice axe after reaching the top of Shepards Pass. You will find that some sections of the ridge will be snow or ice covered and some areas will be free and clear. Move slowly with calculated deliberation across frozen sections. As with the approach to Shepards Pass, snow cover can eliminate the tedious process of stepping from boulder to boulder, making straight-line travel possible. The dangers lie in the quality of the surface. Snow can fall away, causing avalanches. Kick steps into the surface to ensure a solid base to put weight on. Keep your ice axe in your uphill hand in case you slip and need to self-arrest. On your way back down the trail, keep your weight over your center of mass to maintain balance.

Simply follow your footsteps back down to the trail below. Summiting Mount Williamson or descending to the trailhead are your options from this point.

The return hike from Shepards Pass may require you to cross some snow or ice as you start down. Expect to encounter at least a few stretches of frozen ground even late into the season. The use of micro-spikes would be smart. Be mindful of foot placement, as the fall could be catastrophic. In winter and early season, make sure to have crampons and an ice axe for safety.

There will be flowing fresh water along the trail for most of the descent. Anvil Camp is a great place to stop and catch your breath, but be mindful that the mosquitoes are thick during warmer weather. The remaining miles feature views of Mount Williamson and the Owens Valley.

Hiking Information

Closest Outfitters

Big Willi Mountaineering Company, 120 S. Main St., Ste. 13 and 14, Lone Pine, CA 93545; (760) 878-2849; https://bigwillimc.com

Stop in for last-minute supplies and ask Blair about his favorite places to explore in the Sierras. If you are driving north on US 395 from picking up your permit, Big Willi is located just past the stoplight in Lone Pine.

Carroll's Market, 136 S. Main St., Big Pine, CA 93513

Great Pre- or Post-Mountain Spots

Copper Top BBQ, 310 S. Main St., Big Pine, CA 93513; (760) 970-5577; www.coppertopbbq.com

Voted the "Best Barbeque" in the country in 2015, this roadside take-out stand has become a food destination for folks across the country. Huge fan of the tri-tip after a few days in the mountains.

Aberdeen Restaurant, 150 Tinemaha Rd., Independence, CA 93526; (760) 938-2663; www.aberdeenresort.com

Shuttle Service

East Side Shuttle Service, Independence, CA; (760) 878-8047; paul@inyopro.com; www.eastsidesierrashuttle.com

7 Split Mountain

Elevation: 14,058 feet, 10th highest
Start: Red Lake Trailhead
Distance: 14 miles round-trip
Primary route: Red Lake Trail to North Slope
Elevation gain: 7,418 feet
Hiking time: 12 to 18 hours
Difficulty: Class 1, Class 2
Trail surface: Dirt trail leading to talus, exposed scramble
Trailhead elevation: 6,640 feet
Camping: Dispersed camping at trailhead, dispersed camping at Red Lake

Fees: None
Permit: Yes
Best seasons: Summer and fall; technical winter climb
Maps: Tom Harrison Kings Canyon High Country; USGS Split Mountain
Nearest town: Big Pine, CA
Trail contact: White Mountain Ranger Station, 798 N. Main St., Bishop, CA 93514; (619) 873-2500
First ascent: July 23, 1902, Helen and Joseph LeConte

Finding the trailhead: From the corner of US 395 and Crocker Avenue in Big Pine, head west toward the mountains and Glacier Lodge. At 2.5 miles, turn left onto McMurray Road just after you cross Big Pine Creek. This is a dirt road that forks to the left and right immediately after you go up a short incline. Take the left fork, which initially goes to the southeast and then southwest. At 10 miles, turn left onto FR 33E301. At 10.5 miles, reach a creek crossing with steep banks. At 11.1 miles, bear right at a fork toward Tinemaha Creek on FR 33E302. At 11.8 miles, cross Tinemaha Creek. At 14.5 miles, turn right (toward the mountains) on FR 10S01 to the Red Lake Trailhead. At the T-intersection, the kiosk will be 200 feet to your left and the trailhead will be 200 feet to your right. GPS: 37.02080°N / 118.4214°W

The Hike

The southernmost fourteener in the Palisades, Split Mountain's Red Lake Trailhead is the most challenging to reach. The trail itself may, not in difficulty but in definition, be the most frustrating to hike. The difficulty of the drive to the trailhead directly impacts the overall definition of the trail conditions. The Forest Service access roads to the trailhead are rocky, cross several creeks, and require a vehicle with high clearance to manage the terrain. The inaccessibility of getting to the trailhead means that fewer people attempt to climb Split Mountain annually than all of the other fourteeners. Fewer boots on the trail allows the plant growth to overtake sections of the trail, which makes the route difficult at times to follow.

Once you turn off of Glacier Lodge Road outside of Big Pine, the adventure begins. The dirt roads are minimally maintained and at times strewn with sharp rocks waiting to damage tires. It would be a good idea to stash a couple cans of Fix-a-Flat in the vehicle in case of an emergency. It may only be a 15-mile drive, but plan on taking at least an hour to reach the trailhead. Depending on the time of year, the creek crossings may be bone-dry bumper-dragging obstacles or full of rapidly moving

After 4.5 miles on the trail, you will reach the shore of Lower Lake and how Split Mountain got its name comes into view. Do not be surprised to see an abundance of trout in the mountain lakes throughout the Sierras.

The Red Lake Trail can, at times, be a challenge to follow as it meanders up the valley. When in doubt, follow the natural contours and the trail will reappear.

water waiting to stall your car. Roadside assistance will take time to reach you, so be smart with the decisions you make here. To reach the Red Lake Trailhead by motorized vehicle, choose something with four-wheel-drive capabilities since the road will be rocky and loose in places.

Eventually the road will lead you right to the trailhead kiosk and parking area, where you are faced with another decision. There are two distinct trails that head up to Red Lake. The trail behind the kiosk shadows Red Mountain Creek. Unless you want to move at less than 1 mile per hour, want to work on bushwhacking, or are a glutton for mental frustration, *do not* take this route at any cost!

The Red Lake Trail to Red Lake starts 300 feet to the northwest of the kiosk. It is designated by a simple trail sign on a single post. There are a couple of parking spots here, and the sign can be easily hidden by someone's parked car. *This* is the trail you want to take. Leaving the parking area behind, the trail heads up a slight ridgeline before starting a series of long switchbacks. As you turn around the corner and head up the valley, Red Mountain Creek will be about a quarter mile below and on your left.

The trail stays on the right side of the canyon until you reach Red Lake. Due to a lack of foot traffic, there will be points where the trail disappears. Overgrown plants

To reach the final summit approach to Split Mountain, be prepared to scramble through talus above Red Lake. Part of the challenge in reaching the summit from this point will be your route choice. Like the lower trail which disappears at times, the cairns that mark this section are sporadic or, often, nonexistent.

This spot just off the trail was the perfect place to bivy for the night. I started up the trail late in the day with the goal of camping at one of the spots around Red Lake, but after playing hide-and-seek with the trail in the dark, I reached this location just below the tree line and pitched my Big Agnes tent.

will cover and choke the trail, and cairns are virtually nonexistent across the talus fields. Finding and maintaining your route becomes a mental challenge. On the other mountains, the preferred routes receive enough foot traffic that they are permanently defined. You can take a mental vacation, look around, and even snap a photo or two on these trails and not have to worry about the trail still being underfoot. This is not the case with the Red Lake Trail.

It is very easy to wander off the preferred route by mistake during the 5-mile trek to the lake. During the day the trail plays peekaboo, and in the dark of night it can be near impossible to stay on. Fortunately, the trail stays above the creek on the right and follows the natural contours of the land. If you find you are off-trail, cross-country travel here is reasonable. But if you stay focused when you are on-trail, picking it back up should be relatively easy.

There will be some springs and marshy areas to refill water bottles just below the tree line. Be very aware of the cacti around—pulling 75 needles out of the palm of your hand is the result of tripping into one, and that kind of fun is not recommended. Once you reach the lower lake, Split Mountain comes into view, and shortly after that you will reach the banks of Red Lake. Many people treat this hike as a multiday summit approach and set up camp at one of the many sites on the shoreline. The mosquitoes, depending on the season, may keep you sheltered in your tent if you do not pack bug spray.

From Red Lake the push to the summit is visible. Hike along the northeastern bank of the lake until you find the stream that feeds in from the north. Stay to the right of this stream as you gain elevation. The tree line and scrub will give way to talus and boulders. Make upward progress to the plateau above, following the faint trail. Several springs between 11,000 and 12,000 feet provide fresh water. Once you reach the plateau, the saddle between Split Mountain and Mount Prater will come into view.

You might want to break out the micro-spikes you have been carrying, as there will be a snowfield between you and the saddle. How big that snowfield is will depend on the time of year. This bowl receives protection from the sun on three sides, so even in late season there will be some snow to traverse. During early season use trekking poles and crampons to cross here. On the other side of the snow, a section of Class 3 scrambling takes you up to the saddle through a series of loose switchbacks. Once the saddle has been reached, the North Slope approach becomes a straightforward Class 2 hike to the summit.

To the north from the summit, Middle Palisade, Disappointment Peak, and Norman Clyde Peak will all be visible on a clear day. As with all of the mountains in this book, attention needs to be paid to what the skies above are doing. Storms can build quickly in the afternoon, and getting caught on an exposed face can be dangerous. Do not fall victim to summit fever and climb into bad weather. As long as you are still around, the mountain will be here for you to climb. Remember that it takes approximately 1 hour to gain 1,000 feet.

Descending from Split Mountain requires retracing your steps. Later in the day, that snowfield may become soft and slick as the temperature warms. Be mindful and keep your weight back to stay balanced and stable. Minimize the shock to your

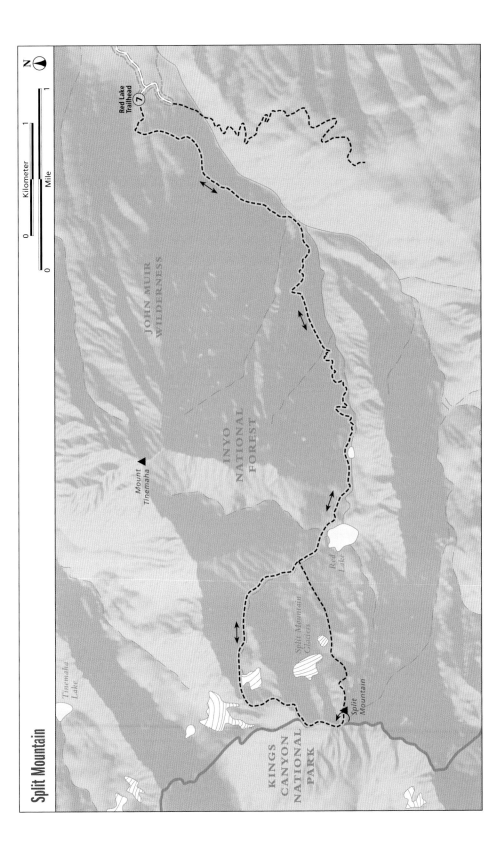

Split Mountain

N

Tinemaha Lake

Mount Tinemaha ▲

JOHN MUIR WILDERNESS

INYO NATIONAL FOREST

Red Lake

Split Mountain Glacier

Split Mountain ▲

KINGS CANYON NATIONAL PARK

Red Lake Trailhead ⑦

Kilometer
0   1   1

Mile
0   1

hips, knees, and ankles by stepping with care as opposed to jumping from boulder to boulder on the way back to Red Lake. The 5 miles back to the trailhead should pass quickly, leaving the tedious drive back to Big Pine as all that stands between you and a celebration dinner at Copper Top BBQ.

Alternate Route: Bishop Pass to Mather Pass via the John Muir Trail/Pacific Crest Trail

Finding the trailhead: Drive south out of Bishop on CA 168. Turn left (east) onto Bishop Creek Road toward South Lake for 8 miles to the trailhead. There are several designated campgrounds along the way; you can reserve a spot in advance through the Recreation.gov site. The trail begins at the south end of the parking area. GPS: 37.1694; -118.5660

This route starts at a higher point (9,825 feet) than the North Fork Big Pine approach 2,000 feet lower. This approach involves a more gradual elevation gain but will require some solid route-finding skills once Bishop Pass has been reached and cross-country travel begins.

South Lake will sit on your right (west) for the first few minutes until you reach a trail junction. Stay on the left trail at this point. Just over a mile down the trail, a side trail that circumnavigates Chocolate Peak will head slightly east. Should you detour down this route, it rejoins with the trail to Bishop Pass after a couple of miles. This is a very cool side trip, and the camping along the Chocolate Lakes provides great views.

To reach Bishop Pass, however, stay on the main trail and pass Long Lake on your right. Just a touch over 5 miles from the trailhead, you will reach Bishop Pass. Dusy Basin will be below you to the south/southwest. Thunderbolt Peak will be visible to the south. Maintain the trail as you descend into Le Conte Canyon. Over the 6.8 miles of hiking, there will be an elevation loss of more than 3,200 feet.

After descending back below the tree line, the Bishop Pass Trail intersects with the combined John Muir and Pacific Crest Trails. While there is a ranger cabin just north of this junction, dispersed camping is allowed all along the route. There are restrictions on having open fires above specific elevations, so please be aware. You will find ample water sources crossing or near the trail. It is always smart to purify drinking and cooking water in the backcountry.

When you reach this junction, turn left (south) and follow the trail for 14 miles. Depending on the time of year, the flies and mosquitoes may be close to unbearable, so do not forget to pack your bug spray. When you camp, make sure to set your bear-proof containers at least 30 feet from your camp.

Mather Pass, at 12,100 feet, will serve as the point where you leave the comfort of the trail and begin cross-country travel. Drop off the trail with Lake 11 as your target. From the lake, head due east to the saddle between Mount Prater and Split Mountain. There will be some talus to negotiate as you climb the 1,000 feet or so to the ridge. Once on the ridgeline, hike south and up the north slope of Split Mountain to the summit. To return to Bishop Pass, simply retrace your steps.

Closest Outfitters

Big Willi Mountaineering Company, 120 S. Main St., Ste. 13 and 14, Lone Pine, CA 93545; (760) 878-2849; https://bigwillimc.com

Stop in for last-minute supplies and ask Blair about his favorite places to explore in the Sierras. If you are driving north on US 395 from picking up your permit, Big Willi is located just past the stoplight in Lone Pine.

Carroll's Market, 136 S. Main St., Big Pine, CA 93513

Great Pre- or Post-Mountain Spots

Copper Top BBQ, 310 S. Main St., Big Pine, CA 93513; (760) 970-5577; www .coppertopbbq.com

Voted the "Best Barbeque" in the country in 2015, this roadside take-out stand has become a food destination for folks across the country. Huge fan of the tri-tip after a few days in the mountains.

Aberdeen Restaurant, 150 Tinemaha Rd., Independence, CA 93526; (760) 938-2663; www.aberdeenresort.com

Shuttle Service

East Side Shuttle Service, Independence, CA; (760) 878-8047; paul@inyopro .com; www.eastsidesierrashuttle.com

8 Middle Palisade

Elevation: 14,108 feet, 13th highest
Start: South Fork Big Pine Creek Trailhead (Glacier Lodge)
Distance: 14 miles round-trip
Primary route: South Fork Big Pine Creek Trailhead to Brainerd Lake to Northeast Face
Elevation gain: 6,212 feet
Hiking time: 12 to 18 hours
Difficulty: Class 1, Class 3/4
Trail surface: Dirt trail leading to talus, glacier travel, moderate exposure
Trailhead elevation: 7,800 feet

Camping: Designated camping at Glacier Lodge campground, dispersed camping at Brainerd Lake
Fees: None
Permit: Yes
Best seasons: Late spring, summer, and fall; technical winter climb
Maps: Tom Harrison The Palisades; USGS Split Mountain
Nearest town: Big Pine, CA
Trail contact: White Mountain Ranger Station, 798 N. Main St., Bishop, CA 93514; (619) 873-2500
First ascent: June 7, 1930, Norman Clyde

Finding the trailhead: From the corner of US 395 and Crocker Avenue in Big Pine, head west toward the mountains and Glacier Lodge. Crocker Avenue becomes Glacier Lodge Road just outside of town. Stay on Glacier Lodge Road for 11 miles until you arrive at the trailhead parking area. GPS: 37.07000°N / 118.4692°W

The Hike

Driving up Glacier Lodge Road to the trailhead below the Palisades, you will be surrounded by tall pines, trout streams, and serenity.

There are two very different ways to reach the South Fork Big Pine Creek Trail. You can walk out of Glacier Lodge Campground, past Glacier Lodge, and up an access road that passes cabins. This will put the creek on your right-hand side, and you will have to cross the water after about a mile to access the South Fork trail. The drier and more direct way to the trail is to use the trailhead located at the kiosk parking area. This keeps the South Fork on your left and also keeps your feet dry!

Follow the access road until the trail breaks off to the right and up the canyon. If you reach the creek while still on the road, you have gone about a quarter mile too far. The trail from here to Brainerd Lake should be easy to follow as it wanders up the valley. You will cross the South Fork of Big Pine Creek a couple of times. There are no bridges on this lower section of the hike, so plan on getting your feet wet. The water will flow fast even in late season, so be mindful as you step, as the rocks can be slick. After the second crossing, the trail heads to the left side of the valley. The smart decision will be to remove your shoes and wade across. This will keep your footwear dry for the upcoming summit!

After hiking up the South Fork Big Pine Creek Trail, camping at Brainerd Lake is the perfect way to recover before your summit attempt. There are several spots along the rocky shoreline that tents fit perfectly in.

From the switchbacks heading up to the headwall, the waterfall created by the South Fork roars into view. The footing will be solid and the trail is a breeze to follow for the next several miles. There will be a couple of talus fields where the trail may not be blatantly obvious. These are short sections where the next step reveals itself just when you think it does not exist. Reaching a small saddle at the top, the flora changes almost immediately.

A beautiful alpine forest awaits you on the other side. You lose a little elevation as you enter the woods, and the shade provided by the pines is a wonderful break from the sun. The trail may become a little soft and muddy in spots, as there is an abundance of water around. This also means that you will likely encounter mosquitoes, so keep your bug spray handy. A log bridge over the creek is a wonderful spot to replenish your water supply. The trail will fork as it rises out of the forest. The options will be Brainerd Lake or Willow Lake. To summit Middle Palisade, choose the Brainerd Lake option.

The trail passes a granite cliff and a tarn just below it. Follow the cairns that lead the way up, over, and around the boulders that protect the water. Middle Palisade will start to creep into view from here. The trail winds its way across a marshy area and

The attack of Middle Palisade from the east winds from the valley below to the glacier before reaching the ridgeline for your summit approach.

From several points along the South Fork Big Pine Creek Trail, Middle Palisade can be seen. After switchbacking through a talus field, you will reach a small pass. The rock formation off to your left is a great place for a quick snack before dropping into a lush alpine forest.

then opens up to the shore of Brainerd Lake. There are several campsites along the rocks on the northwest side of the lake. The designated trail also ends at the lake's edge.

Follow the northern shore of Brainerd to find the cairned route that climbs up the steep talus field to the west. Travel here may be slow. Keep your eyes open to spot the cairns, as they blend into the talus very well. The trail stays to the right-hand side of the boulders and climbs quickly, and the high campsites around Finger Lake and

The maintained trail ends at the shoreline of Brainerd Lake. Follow the cairns around the lake to your right to find the route to Finger Lake.

From the ridge above Finger Lake, the view back to the east showcases Brainerd Lake (near) and Willow Lake as well as the White Mountains on the distant horizon.

Situated at the base of Middle Palisade is the Middle Palisade Glacier. Often it will be more efficient to make the final approach on the glacier instead of hopping through the talus moraine.

the Middle Palisade Glacier will soon be in sight. Be mindful of your route-finding, as the trail is not maintained. This is a great location to camp and prepare for an early morning summit attempt.

You will be able to see the talus rib that splits the Middle Palisade Glacier from Finger Lake. Head up the hill on the west side of Finger Lake and use the switchbacks to reach the moraine below the snow. There will be a slight trail heading southwest past a small glacial tarn. If you have crampons, or are climbing during the early or late season, travel across the snow will be easier than through the talus. Gain the slight ridge in front of you and work toward the grassy area located at the northern end

As the South Fork Big Pine Creek Trail works its way up the valley to Brainerd Lake, there will be several places where boulders impede the direct route. Carefully pick your way through them. Do not bother looking for cairns; the smart play is to look across these short sections and find where the trail picks up on the other side.

of Middle Palisade Glacier's moraine. Stay on this ridge until you reach the base of Middle Palisade.

You should be between a rock moraine on your south side and a rock ridge that separates Middle Palisade Glacier from Norman Clyde Glacier. From here, locate the red rock chute and use the ledges and chimney to scramble up to the gendarme. This section is mostly Class 3, but will require some Class 4 moves to reach the gendarme, which should be on your right side. The summit will be visible to the south. Once

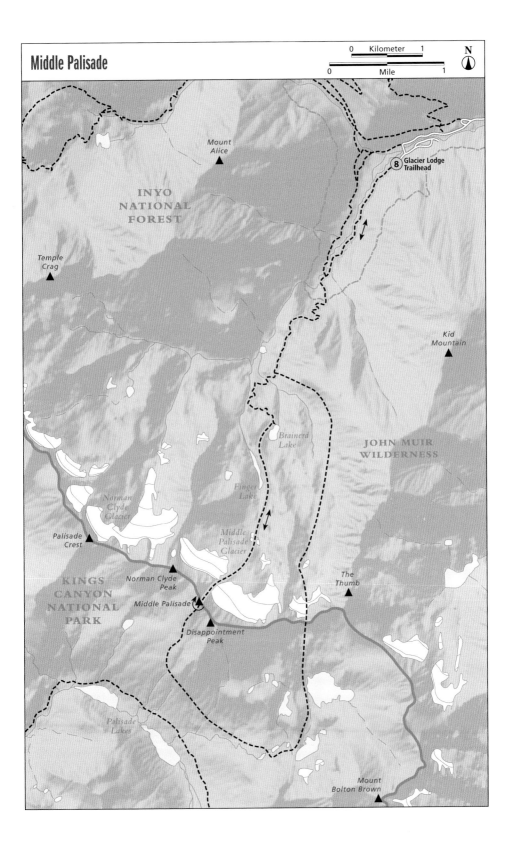

Middle Palisade

Mount
Alice

8 Glacier Lodge
Trailhead

INYO
NATIONAL
FOREST

Temple
Crag

Kid
Mountain

Brainerd
Lake

JOHN MUIR
WILDERNESS

Finger
Lake

Norman
Clyde
Glacier

Palisade
Crest

Middle
Palisade
Glacier

Norman Clyde
Peak

The
Thumb

KINGS
CANYON
NATIONAL
PARK

Middle Palisade

Disappointment
Peak

Palisade
Lakes

Mount
Bolton Brown

out of the chimney, you enter a couloir that will take you the final 500 feet to the peak. When the couloir splits, chose the direction that looks best to you, since they end up on either side of the summit. A few more moves and you will be on top of Middle Palisade. Descend by retracing your steps.

Alternate Route: Traverse from Disappointment Peak (Class 4)

Like the route to the Northeast Face, this hike begins at the Glacier Lodge Campground. Sites here can be reserved in advance and serve as a perfect place to acclimate and prepare for climbing the Palisades.

There are two very different ways to reach the South Fork Big Pine Creek Trail. You can walk out of Glacier Lodge Campground, past Glacier Lodge, and up an access road that passes cabins. This will put the creek on your right-hand side, and you will have to cross the water after about a mile to access the South Fork trail. The drier and more direct way to the trail is to use the trailhead located at the kiosk parking area. This keeps the South Fork on your left and also keeps your feet dry!

Follow the access road until the trail breaks off to the right and up the canyon. If you reach the creek while still on the road, you have gone about a quarter mile too far. The trail from here to Brainerd Lake should be easy to follow as it wanders up the valley. You will cross the South Fork of Big Pine Creek a couple of times. There are no bridges on this lower section of the hike, so plan on getting your feet wet. The water will flow fast even in late season, so be mindful as you step, as the rocks can be slick. After the second crossing, the trail heads to the left side of the valley. The smart decision will be to remove your shoes and wade across. This will keep your footwear dry for the upcoming summit!

From the switchbacks heading up to the headwall, the waterfall created by the South Fork roars into view. The footing will be solid and the trail is a breeze to follow for the next several miles. There will be a couple of talus fields where the trail may not be blatantly obvious. These are short sections where the next step reveals itself just when you think it does not exist. Reaching a small saddle at the top, the flora changes almost immediately.

A beautiful alpine forest awaits you on the other side. You lose a little elevation as you enter the woods, and the shade provided by the pines is a wonderful break from the sun. The trail may become a little soft and muddy in spots, as there is an abundance of water around. This also means that you will likely encounter mosquitoes, so keep your bug spray handy. A log bridge over the creek is a wonderful spot to replenish your water supply. The trail will fork as it rises out of the forest. The options will be Brainerd Lake or Willow Lake. To summit Middle Palisade, choose the Brainerd Lake option.

The trail passes a granite cliff and a tarn just below it. Follow the cairns that lead the way up, over, and around the boulders that protect the water. Middle Palisade will start to creep into view from here. The trail winds its way across a marshy area and then opens up to the shore of Brainerd Lake. There are several campsites along the rocks on the northwest side of the lake. The designated trail also ends at the lake's edge.

Follow the northern shore of Brainerd to find the cairned route that climbs up the steep talus field to the west. Travel here may be slow. Keep your eyes open to spot the cairns, as they blend into the talus very well. The trail stays to the right-hand side of the boulders and climbs quickly, and the high campsites around Finger Lake and the Middle Palisade Glacier will soon be in sight. Be mindful of your route-finding, as the trail is not maintained. This is a great location to camp and prepare for an early morning summit attempt.

Once you have passed Finger Lake, head up the ridgeline to the east toward South-fork Pass. This route is best climbed in the early season when snow and ice cover the moraine field below the pass. Plan on using your ice axe and crampons as you climb the ridge. In later months this route becomes rocky with unpredictable footing.

Finger Lake sits at 10,400 feet. You will gain almost 3,000 feet in just over a mile to reach Southfork Pass. Middle Palisade lies to the northwest. To complete this traverse to the summit, you will be required to climb up and down through six chute-arête combinations. On paper the traverse looks to be very straightforward and smooth, while in reality it is the exact opposite.

Take your time and scout the route ahead of you to ensure that much of this section remains Class 3. You may find at times that the exposure leans toward Class 4 on your way to the summit of Disappointment Peak. Disappointment Peak stands just under 100 feet lower than Middle Palisade, and the two are separated by about a quarter mile of distance.

Descend to the east to the notch between Disappointment Peak and Balcony Peak and then head north. A steep gully drops away to the glacier floor below, so be mindful of where you place your steps on this section.

To cross the gully and continue on to Middle Palisade, you have a few options. If you stay high, there is a slight overhang that will allow you to climb down to solid footing. There is also a Class 4 downclimb that will provide a crossing. Or, you can downclimb into the loose gully and reclimb once you reach the other side. All three routes are viable, and your choice should be based on the skill set of the group you are with.

Once the gully has been crossed, the route begins a gradual ascent. The route takes you just below the ridge across some solid Class 3 terrain. You will reach the ridgeline just short of the summit. Continue along the Class 3 ridge blocks until you reach the summit. Simply retrace your steps back to Southfork Pass and the glacial basin to complete your summit bid.

Closest Outfitters

Big Willi Mountaineering Company, 120 S. Main St., Ste. 13 and 14, Lone Pine, CA 93545; (760) 878-2849; https://bigwillimc.com

Stop in for last-minute supplies and ask Blair about his favorite places to explore in the Sierras. If you are driving north on US 395 from picking up your permit, Big Willi is located just past the stoplight in Lone Pine.

Carroll's Market, 136 S. Main St., Big Pine, CA 93513

Great Pre- or Post-Mountain Spots

Copper Top BBQ, 310 S. Main St., Big Pine, CA 93513; (760) 970-5577; www .coppertopbbq.com

Voted the "Best Barbeque" in the country in 2015, this roadside take-out stand has become a food destination for folks across the country. Huge fan of the tri-tip after a few days in the mountains.

Aberdeen Restaurant, 150 Tinemaha Rd., Independence, CA 93526; (760) 938-2663; www.aberdeenresort.com

Shuttle Service

East Side Shuttle Service, Independence, CA; (760) 878-8047; paul@inyopro .com; www.eastsidesierrashuttle.com

9 Thunderbolt Peak

Elevation: 14,003 feet, 15 highest
Start: North Fork Big Pine Creek Trailhead
(Glacier Lodge)
Distance: 22 miles round-trip
Primary route: North Fork Big Pine Creek Trail-
head to Glacier Trail to Southwest Chute
Elevation gain: 6,203 feet
Hiking time: 12 to 18 hours
Difficulty: Class 1, Class 4/5
Trail surface: Dirt trail leading to talus, glacier
travel, high exposure with 5.10 summit block
Trailhead elevation: 7,800 feet
Camping: Designated camping at Glacier Lodge
campground, dispersed camping along trail

Fees: None
Permit: Yes
Best seasons: Late spring, summer, and fall;
technical winter climb
Maps: Tom Harrison The Palisades, Bishop
Pass North Lake–South Lake Loop; USGS North
Palisade
Nearest town: Big Pine, CA
Trail contact: White Mountain Ranger Station,
798 N. Main St., Bishop, CA 93514; (619)
873-2500
First ascent: August 13, 1931, Glen Dawson
and Jules Eichorn

Finding the trailhead: From the corner of US 395 and Crocker Avenue in Big Pine, head west toward the mountains and Glacier Lodge. Crocker Avenue becomes Glacier Lodge Road just outside of town. Stay on Glacier Lodge Road for 11 miles until you arrive at the trailhead parking area. GPS: 37.07000°N / 118.4692°W

The Hike

When eight legendary climbers set out to climb what is now known as Thunderbolt Peak for the first time in 1931, they were hoping to summit the last of the California fourteeners. During the month of August, clouds can build into thunderstorms very rapidly, and this day was typical. Two of the eight had managed to scale the summit block as the storm started whipping up. Seeking what little shelter was available, the group huddled together as a lightning bolt struck the monolith above them. Once the storm passed, the remaining members of the group summited the aptly named Thunderbolt Peak.

North Couloir (Northeast Couloir, Northeast Buttress) via North Fork Big Pine
From the parking area, head west onto the trail. There will be some cabins on the right above you. Cross the bridge over the North Fork and follow this well-used trail to a junction that offers the "upper trail" option. Your choice here is easy. You can take the shorter and steeper upper trail or stay in the valley on the lower one. They will end up in the exact same spot 2 miles up the trail. The lower trail follows an access road, while the upper route is a rocky singletrack. When the two converge, the trail starts to switchback toward Second Falls and will stay to the right of the tumbling

Thunderbolt Peak, the most technical of California's Fourteeners, looms dauntingly during the cross-country approach from Bishop Pass. This route sets the climber up to complete the Palisades Traverse consisting of Thunderbolt Peak, Starlight Peak, North Palisade, Polemonium Peak, and Mount Sill.

North Fork. While this is a very photogenic part of the trail, do not wander too close to the water while capturing the moment.

About a mile later you will pass the ranger's cabin on the left side of the trail. The North Fork flows gently by the covered porch of the cabin, providing a shaded and sheltered spot to catch your breath or escape the weather. Be mindful that this is an active bear area. Please read the section in the introduction that details how to handle your food stores and face-to-face encounters with black bears in the Sierras. It is not uncommon to see scratch marks in trees.

Between the cabin and First Lake, the travel will be smooth and easy. The smooth dirt trail only gains 2,000 feet over these 6 miles as it meanders through the woods. The North Fork will almost always be in sight on this section, which means that a fresh water source will be readily available. It would be smart to filter or purify any water at this stage, since the animal and human traffic can be high. On-trail left, Mount Alice and Temple Crag will come into view between the trees.

The mountain lakes that you will encounter are numbered like the waterfalls: First, Second, Third, and so on. This makes it easy to stay in your map and know exactly where you are. The trail junctions are also clearly marked with directional signs to keep you on route. Those looking to camp will find sites with both protection and incredible views along the shorelines. The first three lakes all sit at around 10,000 feet in elevation and are less than 2 miles apart. There are some incredible sites around each lake. In addition to the lakes, there are several small streams and springs along the trail for water.

Just past Third Lake the trail steepens and switchbacks for a period before the Glacier Trail junction. You will want to choose the Glacier Trail heading to the left. This trail may seem less maintained and slightly overgrown compared to the North Fork Trail to this point, a result of lower levels of foot traffic. The trail drops down ever so slightly in elevation as it heads back into the trees and into a marshy meadow. Stay on the rock walkway through this area to help reduce soil erosion and damage.

The tree line will slowly give way as the trail becomes rocky and somewhat loose. You will only need a mile on the Glacier Trail to enter into the green space that comprises Sam Mack Meadow. Below Sam Mack Lake the meadow features a gently rolling stream (unless you are there during early season when the snow is melting) cutting right down the middle. The trail crosses the stream via boulders left by glacial erosion. If you camp here, be mindful of the mosquitoes!

After crossing the stream, the trail climbs steeply up the cliff to the ridge to the southeast in front of you. Expect the footing to be loose in places as you traverse around the cliff. Once you come around the corner, all five summits come into view for the first time. Climbing up and over a ridge, the trail will eventually disappear as the glacial moraine begins to dominate the land. Traverse the moraine east toward the northwest ridge of Mount Gayley until it combines with the Palisade Glacier's terminal moraine. The talus field can be crossed easily during early season, but when

Looking back on the Big Pine Lakes from above Sam Mack Meadow.

the snow has melted, it becomes challenging both physically and mentally. You will be able to see the prominent North Couloir and your route to the ridgeline.

Make your way up the 1,000 feet through the couloir. Expect to encounter snow and ice during all seasons. Having the snow cover will aid in the crossing of talus but may require ice tools to safely navigate. Stay to the left side as you approach the ridgeline. Expect this section to take up to two hours to complete.

From the approach from the Palisade Glacier below to the final summit block, Thunderbolt Peak requires the most skill and subjects the climber to the most exposure of any of the California fourteeners. Follow the Glacier Trail up the ridge east of the meadow as described above to reach the glacier. Continue along the ridge above the Palisade Glacier's moraine field. The talus field can be crossed easily during early season, but when the snow has melted, it becomes challenging both physically and mentally.

At the top of the ridge, you will need to traverse down to the saddle below Thunderbolt's northeast ridge. You will see a pair of chutes in front of you. Take the more direct path to the southernmost chute. Following the chute takes you to the notch between Thunderbolt and Starlight. During the early season you can stay on the snow in the chute, but later in the season the best route will be to stay on the rocks (Class 3/4) on the sides. The loose footing left after the snow has melted can be challenging to climb.

Once you reach the notch that separates the two peaks, you will work up through the Class 3 slabs toward the summit. Traverse the right side of the ridge and around the corner of a headwall. Negotiating the corner requires some very exposed Class 4 moves to gain the steep blocks that take you to a flat area where you can catch your breath.

From here the summit block is just a few steps away. This is the point where the "pucker factor" really hits you. As if the challenging climb to get within feet of the summit was not enough, the series of 5.8–5.10 moves you will have to execute in order to stand on the peak will get your heart racing.

The final few feet to the summit are completely exposed, and only the very skilled should attempt to reach the block without aid. The rope, climbing harness, and rappel device that have been weighing down your pack to this point are going to be vital for a safe summit and descent.

After tying one end of your rope to a boulder below the summit block, stand on the formation on the east side of the block. To make the last few feet of climbing a little easier, you can tie a series of bight knots in the rope to be used for grip while climbing hand over hand. Attach the loose end of the rope to your harness with a carabiner so that you do not lose the rope in the wind.

Lasso the summit by throwing the rope up and over to provide stable and safe aid to the summit. Start the final moves by stepping onto the boulders below the summit and begin climbing up the rope one knot at a time. If the conditions warrant, you can clip into the bights with a carabiner for extra protection. After the true summit has

The Palisades: Thunderbolt, Starlight, North Palisade, Polemonium and Mount Sill

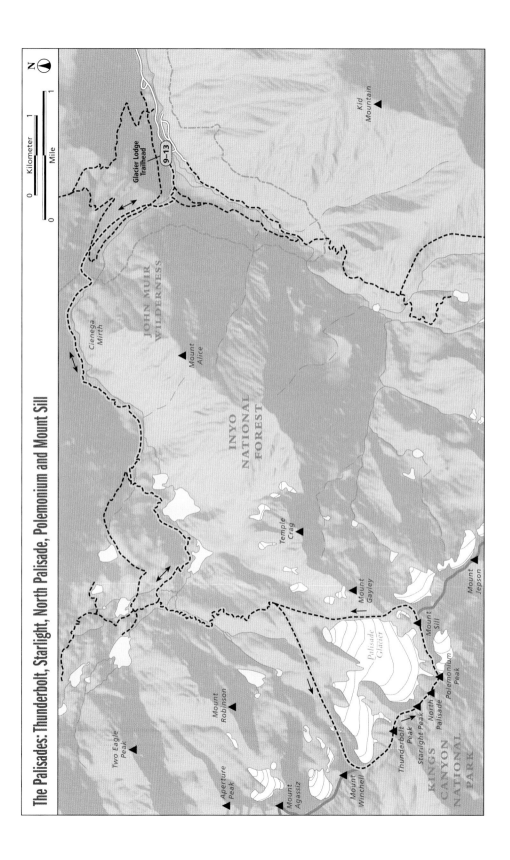

Two Eagle Peak

Aperture Peak

Mount Robinson

Mount Agassiz

Mount Winchell

Thunderbolt Peak

Starlight Peak

North Palisade

Polemonium Peak

Palisade Glacier

Mount Sill

Mount Gayley

Mount Jepson

Temple Crag

KINGS CANYON NATIONAL PARK

INYO NATIONAL FOREST

JOHN MUIR WILDERNESS

Cienega Mirth

Mount Alice

Kid Mountain

Glacier Lodge Trailhead

9-13

N

been reached, downclimb or rappel back to the boulders below, gather your rope and gear, and do one of two things: You can retrace your steps back down to the glacier below and to the east, or you can make the traverse to Starlight Peak.

Alternate Route: Bishop Pass

Finding the trailhead: Drive south out of Bishop on CA 168. Turn left (east) onto Bishop Creek Road toward South Lake for eight miles until you reach the trailhead. There are several designated campgrounds along the way; you can reserve a spot in advance through the Recreation.gov site. The trail begins at the south end of the parking area. GPS: 37.1694; -118.5660

This route starts at a higher point (9,825 feet) than the North Fork Big Pine approach 2,000 lower. This approach involves a more gradual elevation gain but will require some solid route-finding skills once Bishop Pass has been reached and cross-country travel begins.

South Lake will sit on your right (west) for the first few minutes until you reach a trail junction. Stay on the left trail at this point. Just over a mile down the trail, a side trail that circumnavigates Chocolate Peak will head slightly east. Should you detour down this route, it rejoins with the trail to Bishop Pass after a couple of miles. This is a very cool side trip, and the camping along the Chocolate Lakes provides great views.

To reach Bishop Pass, however, stay on the main trail and pass Long Lake on your right. Just a touch over 5 miles from the trailhead, you will reach Bishop Pass. Dusy Basin will be below you to the south/southwest. The first view of Thunderbolt Peak will be along the ridge directly south of the pass. From this point on, you will be hiking across open ground and will need to navigate your way.

Leaving the trail just below the pass, the goal will be to traverse a contour below Mount Agassiz and Mount Winchell but above the talus lining the basin. Try to maintain an elevation close to 12,000 feet as a guideline. There is a sweet spot between the talus above and the talus below as far as the energy expenditure required. Set a bearing on the saddle between Mount Winchell and Thunderbolt Peak. After picking your way through the upper basin for 2.5 miles, Thunderbolt Pass will be reached (approximately 12,000 feet).

At the top of the ridge, you will need to traverse down to the saddle below Thunderbolt's northeast ridge. You will see a pair of chutes in front of you. Take the more direct path to the southernmost chute. Following the chute takes you to the notch between Thunderbolt and Starlight. During the early season you can stay on the snow in the chute, but later in the season the best route will be to stay on the rocks (Class 3/4) on the sides. The loose footing left after the snow has melted can be challenging to climb.

Once you reach the notch that separates the two peaks, you will work up through the Class 3 slabs toward the summit. Traverse the right side of the ridge and around the corner of a headwall. Negotiating the corner requires some very exposed Class 4 moves to gain the steep blocks that take you to a flat area that you can catch your breath at.

Crossing fields of talus is a necessary task to reach the base of each mountain.

From here the summit block is just a few steps away. This is the point where the "pucker factor" really hits you. As if the challenging climb to get within feet of the summit was not enough, the series of 5.8–5.10 moves you will have to execute in order to stand on the peak will get your heart racing.

The final few feet to the summit are completely exposed, and only the very skilled should attempt to reach the block without aid. The rope, climbing harness, and rappel device that have been weighing down your pack to this point are going to be vital for a safe summit and descent.

After tying one end of your rope to a boulder below the summit block, stand on the formation on the east side of the block. To make the last few feet of climbing a little easier, you can tie a series of bight knots in the rope to be used for grip while climbing hand over hand. Attach the loose end of the rope to your harness with a carabiner so that you do not lose the rope in the wind.

Lasso the summit by throwing the rope up and over to provide stable and safe aid to the summit. Start the final moves by stepping onto the boulders below the summit and begin climbing up the rope one knot at a time. If the conditions warrant, you can clip into the bights with a carabiner for extra protection. After the true summit has been reached, downclimb or rappel back to the boulders below, gather your rope and gear, and do one of two things: You can retrace your steps back to Bishop Pass, or you can make the traverse to Starlight Peak.

Hiking Information

Closest Outfitters

Big Willi Mountaineering Company, 120 S. Main St., Ste. 13 and 14, Lone Pine, CA 93545; (760) 878-2849; https://bigwillimc.com

Stop in for last-minute supplies and ask Blair about his favorite places to explore in the Sierras. If you are driving north on US 395 from picking up your permit, Big Willi is located just past the stoplight in Lone Pine.

Carroll's Market, 136 S. Main St., Big Pine, CA 93513

Great Pre- or Post-Mountain Spots

Copper Top BBQ, 310 S. Main St., Big Pine, CA 93513; (760) 970-5577; www .coppertopbbq.com

Voted the "Best Barbeque" in the country in 2015, this roadside take-out stand has become a food destination for folks across the country. Huge fan of the tri-tip after a few days in the mountains.

Aberdeen Restaurant, 150 Tinemaha Rd., Independence, CA 93526; (760) 938-2663; www.aberdeenresort.com

Shuttle Service

East Side Shuttle Service, Independence, CA; (760) 878-8047; paul@inyopro .com; ww.eastsidesierrashuttle.com

10 Starlight Peak

Elevation: 14,220 feet, 5th highest
Start: North Fork Big Pine Creek Trailhead (Glacier Lodge)
Distance: 23 miles round-trip
Primary route: North Fork Big Pine Creek Trailhead to Glacier Trail to traverse from Thunderbolt Peak
Elevation gain: 6,420 feet
Hiking time: 12 to 18 hours
Difficulty: Class 1, Class 4/5
Trail surface: Dirt trail leading to talus, glacier travel, high ridgeline exposure
Trailhead elevation: 7,800 feet

Camping: Designated camping at Glacier Lodge campground, dispersed camping along trail
Fees: None
Permit: Yes
Best seasons: Late spring, summer, and fall; technical winter climb
Maps: Tom Harrison The Palisades, Bishop Pass North Lake–South Lake Loop; USGS North Palisade
Nearest town: Big Pine, CA
Trail contact: White Mountain Ranger Station, 798 N. Main St., Bishop, CA 93514; (619) 873-2500
First ascent: 1930, Norman Clyde

Finding the trailhead: From the corner of US 395 and Crocker Avenue in Big Pine, head west toward the mountains and Glacier Lodge. Crocker Avenue becomes Glacier Lodge Road just outside of town. Stay on Glacier Lodge Road for 11 miles until you arrive at the trailhead parking area. GPS: 37.07000°N / 118.4692°W

The Hike

From the parking area, head west onto the trail. There will be some cabins on the right above you. Cross the bridge over the North Fork and follow this well-used trail to a junction that offers the "upper trail" option. Your choice here is easy. You can take the shorter and steeper upper trail or stay in the valley on the lower one. They will end up in the exact same spot 2 miles up the trail. The lower trail follows an access road, while the upper route is a rocky singletrack. When the two converge, the trail starts to switchback toward Second Falls and will stay to the right of the tumbling North Fork. While this is a very photogenic part of the trail, do not wander too close to the water while capturing the moment.

About a mile later you will pass the ranger's cabin on the left side of the trail. The North Fork flows gently by the covered porch of the cabin, providing a shaded and sheltered spot to catch your breath or escape the weather. Be mindful that this is an active bear area. Please read the section in the introduction that details how to handle your food stores and face-to-face encounters with black bears in the Sierras. It is not uncommon to see scratch marks in trees.

Between the cabin and First Lake, the travel will be smooth and easy. The smooth dirt trail only gains 2,000 feet over these 6 miles as it meanders through the woods. The North Fork will almost always be in sight on this section, which means that a

The Palisades Crest includes some of the Fourteeners most challenging summits. Completing the multiple summit traverse is considered a massive feat by many of the locals.

fresh water source will be readily available. It would be smart to filter or purify any water at this stage, since the animal and human traffic can be high. On-trail left, Mount Alice and Temple Crag will come into view between the trees.

The mountain lakes that you will encounter are numbered like the waterfalls: First, Second, Third, and so on. This makes it easy to stay in your map and know exactly where you are. The trail junctions are also clearly marked with directional signs to keep you on route. Those looking to camp will find sites with both protection and incredible views along the shorelines. The first three lakes all sit at around 10,000 feet in elevation and are less than 2 miles apart. There are some incredible sites around each lake. In addition to the lakes, there are several small streams and springs along the trail for water.

Just past Third Lake the trail steepens and switchbacks for a period before the Glacier Trail junction. You will want to choose the Glacier Trail heading to the left. This trail may seem less maintained and slightly overgrown compared to the North

Fork Trail to this point, a result of lower levels of foot traffic. The trail drops down ever so slightly in elevation as it heads back into the trees and into a marshy meadow. Stay on the rock walkway through this area to help reduce soil erosion and damage.

The tree line will slowly give way as the trail becomes rocky and somewhat loose. You will only need a mile on the Glacier Trail to enter into the green space that comprises Sam Mack Meadow. Below Sam Mack Lake the meadow features a gently rolling stream (unless you are there during early season when the snow is melting) cutting right down the middle. The trail crosses the stream via boulders left by glacial erosion. If you camp here, be mindful of the mosquitoes!

After crossing the stream, the trail climbs steeply up the cliff to the ridge to the southeast in front of you. Expect the footing to be loose in places as you traverse around the cliff. Once you come around the corner, all five summits come into view for the first time. Climbing up and over a ridge, the trail will eventually disappear as the glacial moraine begins to dominate the land. Traverse the moraine east toward the northwest ridge of Mount Gayley until it combines with the Palisade Glacier's terminal moraine. The talus field can be crossed easily during early season, but when the snow has melted, it becomes challenging both physically and mentally. You will be able to see the prominent North Couloir and your route to the ridgeline.

Make your way up the 1,000 feet through the couloir. Expect to encounter snow and ice during all seasons. Having the snow cover will aid in the crossing of talus but may require ice tools to safely navigate. Stay to the left side as you approach the ridgeline. Expect this section to take up to two hours to complete.

From the approach from the Palisade Glacier below to the final summit block, Thunderbolt Peak requires the most skill and subjects the climber to the most exposure of any of the California fourteeners. Follow the Glacier Trail up the ridge east of the meadow as described above to reach the glacier. Continue along the ridge above the Palisade Glacier's moraine field. The talus field can be crossed easily during early season, but when the snow has melted, it becomes challenging both physically and mentally.

At the top of the ridge, you will need to traverse down to the saddle below Thunderbolt's northeast ridge. You will see a pair of chutes in front of you. Take the more direct path to the southernmost chute. Following the chute takes you to the notch between Thunderbolt and Starlight. During the early season you can stay on the snow in the chute, but later in the season the best route will be to stay on the rocks (Class 3/4) on the sides. The loose footing left after the snow has melted can be challenging to climb.

Once you reach the notch that separates the two peaks, you will work up through the Class 3 slabs toward the summit. Traverse the right side of the ridge and around the corner of a headwall. Negotiating the corner requires some very exposed Class 4 moves to gain the steep blocks that take you to a flat area where you can catch your breath. Continue south along the ridge to approach Starlight Peak.

After reaching the notch between Thunderbolt and Starlight Peak via the northeast ridge route described above, you have two distinct route options. Maintaining the ridge crest to Starlight is one. You can also move southwest of the ridge and traverse until the northwest face of Starlight is met. Keep your eyes on the spire to make sure to stay on route.

The milk bottle summit block of Starlight, with a 5.4 rating, is visually intimidating as you stand below it. For aided protection over the last few feet, your rope can be thrown over the "back" of the spire from the east. Again, the impressive summit can be gained using the hand-over-hand approach.

The final moves can be completed without protection. In his book *California's Fourteeners,* Sean O'Rourke describes the spire as being "shaped like a giraffe" and the method of reaching the summit as "pull up onto its rump, then make your way north to its neck. Once at the neck, grasp it and carefully stand up, then make a couple of steep moves to sit on top."

To return to the Glacier Trail approach simply follow the northeast ridge past Thunderbolt Peak and descend down the couloir to the valley below. Alternatively you can proceed to North Palisade and continue the multi-summit traverse.

Climbing a fourteener during the winter or spring provides a great challenge. Always be prepared for potential weather shifts and changes before you start up the trail. Keep a lookout at the ridge-lines above you, as storms can move in quickly.

Alternate Route: Bishop Pass

Finding the trailhead: Drive south out of Bishop on CA 168. Turn left (east) onto Bishop Creek Road toward South Lake for eight miles to the trailhead. There are several designated campgrounds along the way; you can reserve a spot in advance through the Recreation.gov site. The trail begins at the south end of the parking area. GPS: 37.1694; -118.5660

This route starts at a higher point (9,825 feet) than the North Fork Big Pine approach 2,000 feet lower. This approach involves a more gradual elevation gain but will require some solid route-finding skills once Bishop Pass has been reached and cross-country travel begins.

South Lake will sit on your right (west) for the first few minutes until you reach a trail junction. Stay on the left trail at this point. Just over a mile down the trail, a side trail that circumnavigates Chocolate Peak will head slightly east. Should you detour down this route, it rejoins with the trail to Bishop Pass after a couple of miles. This is a very cool side trip, and the camping along the Chocolate Lakes provides great views.

To reach Bishop Pass, however, stay on the main trail and pass Long Lake on your right. Just a touch over 5 miles from the trailhead, you will reach Bishop Pass. Dusy Basin will be below you to the south/southwest. The first view of Thunderbolt Peak will be along the ridge directly south of the pass. From this point on, you will be hiking across open ground and will need to navigate your way.

Leaving the trail just below the pass, the goal will be to traverse a contour below Mount Agassiz and Mount Winchell but above the talus lining the basin. Try to maintain an elevation close to 12,000 feet as a guideline. There is a sweet spot between the talus above and the talus below as far as the energy expenditure required. Set a bearing on the saddle between Mount Winchell and Thunderbolt Peak. After picking your way through the upper basin for 2.5 miles, Thunderbolt Pass will be reached (approximately 12,000 feet).

At the top of the ridge, you will need to traverse down to the saddle below Thunderbolt's northeast ridge. You will see a pair of chutes in front of you. Take the more direct path to the southernmost chute. Following the chute takes you to the notch between Thunderbolt and Starlight. During the early season you can stay on the snow in the chute, but later in the season the best route will be to stay on the rocks (Class 3/4) on the sides. The loose footing left after the snow has melted can be challenging to climb.

Once you reach the notch that separates the two peaks, you will work up through the Class 3 slabs toward the summit. Traverse the right side of the ridge and around the corner of a headwall. Negotiating the corner requires some very exposed Class 4 moves to gain the steep blocks that take you to a flat area that you can catch your breath at. Traverse around Thunderbolt Peak's summit block south toward Starlight Peak.

After reaching the notch between Thunderbolt and Starlight Peak via the northeast ridge route described above, you have two distinct route options. Maintaining the ridge crest to Starlight is one. You can also move southwest of the ridge and traverse until the northwest face of Starlight is met. Keep your eyes on the spire to make sure to stay on route.

The milk bottle summit block of Starlight, with a 5.4 rating, is visually intimidating as you stand below it. For aided protection over the last few feet, your rope can be thrown over the "back" of the spire from the east. Again, the impressive summit can be gained using the hand-over-hand approach.

The final moves can be completed without protection. In his book *California's Fourteeners*, Sean O'Rourke describes the spire as being "shaped like a giraffe" and the method of reaching the summit as "pull up onto its rump, then make your way north to its neck. Once at the neck, grasp it and carefully stand up, then make a couple of steep moves to sit on top."

To return to the Bishop Pass approach simply follow the northeast ridge past Thunderbolt Peak and descend down the couloir to the valley below. Alternatively you can proceed to Polemonium Peak and continue the multi-summit traverse.

Hiking Information

Closest Outfitters

Big Willi Mountaineering Company, 120 S. Main St., Ste. 13 and 14, Lone Pine, CA 93545; (760) 878-2849; https://bigwillimc.com

Stop in for last-minute supplies and ask Blair about his favorite places to explore in the Sierras. If you are driving north on US 395 from picking up your permit, Big Willi is located just past the stoplight in Lone Pine.

Carroll's Market, 136 S. Main St., Big Pine, CA 93513

Great Pre- or Post-Mountain Spots

Copper Top BBQ, 310 S. Main St., Big Pine, CA 93513; (760) 970-5577; www.coppertopbbq.com

Voted the "Best Barbeque" in the country in 2015, this roadside take-out stand has become a food destination for folks across the country. Huge fan of the tri-tip after a few days in the mountains.

Aberdeen Restaurant, 150 Tinemaha Rd., Independence, CA 93526; (760) 938-2663; www.aberdeenresort.com

Shuttle Service

East Side Shuttle Service, Independence, CA; (760) 878-8047; paul@inyopro.com; ww.eastsidesierrashuttle.com

11 North Palisade

Elevation: 14,242 feet, 4th highest
Start: North Fork Big Pine Creek Trailhead (Glacier Lodge)
Distance: 24 miles round-trip
Primary route: North Fork Big Pine Creek Trailhead to Glacier Trail to traverse from Starlight Peak
Elevation gain: 6,422 feet
Hiking time: 12 to 18 hours
Difficulty: Class 1, Class 4/5
Trail surface: Dirt trail leading to talus, glacier travel, high ridgeline exposure
Trailhead elevation: 7,800 feet
Camping: Designated camping at Glacier Lodge campground, dispersed camping along trail

Fees: None
Permit: Yes
Best seasons: Late spring, summer, and fall; technical winter climb
Maps: Tom Harrison The Palisades, Bishop Pass North Lake–South Lake Loop; USGS North Palisade
Nearest town: Big Pine, CA
Trail contact: White Mountain Ranger Station, 798 N. Main St., Bishop, CA 93514; (619) 873-2500
First ascent: July 24, 1903, Joseph LeConte, James Moffitt, James Hutchinson, and Robert Pike

Finding the trailhead: From the corner of US 395 and Crocker Avenue in Big Pine, head west toward the mountains and Glacier Lodge. Crocker Avenue becomes Glacier Lodge Road just outside of town. Stay on Glacier Lodge Road for 11 miles until you arrive at the trailhead parking area. GPS: 37.07000°N / 118.4692°W

The Hike

From the parking area, head west onto the trail. There will be some cabins on the right above you. Cross the bridge over the North Fork and follow this well-used trail to a junction that offers the "upper trail" option. Your choice here is easy. You can take the shorter and steeper upper trail or stay in the valley on the lower one. They will end up in the exact same spot 2 miles up the trail. The lower trail follows an access road, while the upper route is a rocky singletrack. When the two converge, the trail starts to switchback toward Second Falls and will stay to the right of the tumbling North Fork. While this is a very photogenic part of the trail, do not wander too close to the water while capturing the moment.

About a mile later you will pass the ranger's cabin on the left side of the trail. The North Fork flows gently by the covered porch of the cabin, providing a shaded and sheltered spot to catch your breath or escape the weather. Be mindful that this is an active bear area. Please read the section in the introduction that details how to handle your food stores and face-to-face encounters with black bears in the Sierras. It is not uncommon to see scratch marks in trees.

Between the cabin and First Lake, the travel will be smooth and easy. The smooth dirt trail only gains 2,000 feet over these 6 miles as it meanders through the woods.

Located in the middle of the Palisades Crest, a successful summit of North Palisade will earn you bragging rights back at camp.

The North Fork will almost always be in sight on this section, which means that a fresh water source will be readily available. It would be smart to filter or purify any water at this stage, since the animal and human traffic can be high. On-trail left, Mount Alice and Temple Crag will come into view between the trees.

The mountain lakes that you will encounter are numbered like the waterfalls: First, Second, Third, and so on. This makes it easy to stay in your map and know exactly where you are. The trail junctions are also clearly marked with directional signs to keep you on route. Those looking to camp will find sites with both protection and incredible views along the shorelines. The first three lakes all sit at around 10,000 feet in elevation and are less than 2 miles apart. There are some incredible sites around each lake. In addition to the lakes, there are several small streams and springs along the trail for water.

Just past Third Lake the trail steepens and switchbacks for a period before the Glacier Trail junction. You will want to choose the Glacier Trail heading to the left. This trail may seem less maintained and slightly overgrown compared to the North Fork Trail to this point, a result of lower levels of foot traffic. The trail drops down ever so slightly in elevation as it heads back into the trees and into a marshy meadow. Stay on the rock walkway through this area to help reduce soil erosion and damage.

The tree line will slowly give way as the trail becomes rocky and somewhat loose. You will only need a mile on the Glacier Trail to enter into the green space that comprises Sam Mack Meadow. Below Sam Mack Lake the meadow features a gently rolling stream (unless you are there during early season when the snow is melting) cutting right down the middle. The trail crosses the stream via boulders left by glacial erosion. If you camp here, be mindful of the mosquitoes!

After crossing the stream, the trail climbs steeply up the cliff to the ridge to the southeast in front of you. Expect the footing to be loose in places as you traverse around the cliff. Once you come around the corner, all five summits come into view for the first time. Climbing up and over a ridge, the trail will eventually disappear as the glacial moraine begins to dominate the land. Traverse the moraine east toward the northwest ridge of Mount Gayley until it combines with the Palisade Glacier's terminal moraine. The talus field can be crossed easily during early season, but when the snow has melted, it becomes challenging both physically and mentally. You will be able to see the prominent North Couloir and your route to the ridgeline.

Make your way up the 1,000 feet through the couloir. Expect to encounter snow and ice during all seasons. Having the snow cover will aid in the crossing of talus but may require ice tools to safely navigate. Stay to the left side as you approach the ridgeline. Expect this section to take up to two hours to complete.

At the top of the ridge, you will need to traverse down to the saddle below Thunderbolt's northeast ridge. You will see a pair of chutes in front of you. Take the more direct path to the southernmost chute. Following the chute takes you to the notch between Thunderbolt and Starlight. During the early season you can stay on the snow in the chute, but later in the season the best route will be to stay on the rocks (Class

3/4) on the sides. The loose footing left after the snow has melted can be challenging to climb.

Once you reach the notch that separates the two peaks, you will work up through the Class 3 slabs toward the summit. Traverse the right side of the ridge and around the corner of a headwall. Negotiating the corner requires some very exposed Class 4 moves to gain the steep blocks that take you to a flat area where you can catch your breath. Continue south along the ridge to approach Starlight Peak.

After reaching the notch between Thunderbolt and Starlight Peak via the northeast ridge route described above, you have two distinct route options. Maintaining the ridge crest to Starlight is one. You can also move southwest of the ridge and traverse until the northwest face of Starlight is met. Keep your eyes on the spire to make sure to stay on route.

Passing the summit block of Starlight Peak, only a few hundred meters separates you from the summit of North Palisade. The traverse between the two will be Class 4/5 almost the entire way.

From Starlight, hike south down the ridge. You will have to negotiate some large boulders in order to reach the ridge and then a couple of very exposed moves to reach better terrain. Maintain a route on the south side of the ridge and saddle while the travel is easy. Once the route becomes challenging and a gap in the ridge is reached, cross to the north side of the ridge and descend to the west to a point where the gap can be crossed and travel to the east can resume.

Climb up to the platform on the east side. Skilled climbers can use a rope to swing to this platform, instead of using the Class 4/5 traverse, to gain the east side of the gap. Continue up the ridgeline to a chimney just below North Palisade's summit. Turn west and climb through the blocks to reach the summit. Once on the summit, retrace your route north and back to the Palisade Glacier below or continue south on the ridge to Polemonium Peak.

Alternate Route: Bishop Pass

Finding the trailhead: Drive south out of Bishop on CA 168. Turn left (east) onto Bishop Creek Road toward South Lake for eight miles until you reach the trailhead. There are several designated campgrounds along the way; you can reserve a spot in advance through the Recreation.gov site. The trail begins at the south end of the parking area. GPS: 37.1694; -118.5660

This route starts at a higher point (9,825 feet) than the North Fork Big Pine approach 2,000 feet lower. This approach involves a more gradual elevation gain but will require some solid route-finding skills once Bishop Pass has been reached and cross-country travel begins.

South Lake will sit on your right (west) for the first few minutes until you reach a trail junction. Stay on the left trail at this point. Just over a mile down the trail, a side trail that circumnavigates Chocolate Peak will head slightly east. Should you detour down this route, it rejoins with the trail to Bishop Pass after a couple of miles. This is a very cool side trip, and the camping along the Chocolate Lakes provides great views.

Crossing through Sam Mack Meadow on the way to the base of Palisade Glacier.

To reach Bishop Pass, however, stay on the main trail and pass Long Lake on your right. Just a touch over 5 miles from the trailhead, you will reach Bishop Pass. Dusy Basin will be below you to the south/southwest. The first view of Thunderbolt Peak will be along the ridge directly south of the pass. From this point on, you will be hiking across open ground and will need to navigate your way.

Leaving the trail just below the pass, the goal will be to traverse a contour below Mount Agassiz and Mount Winchell but above the talus lining the basin. Try to maintain an elevation close to 12,000 feet as a guideline. There is a sweet spot between the talus above and the talus below as far as the energy expenditure required. Set a bearing on the saddle between Mount Winchell and Thunderbolt Peak. After picking your way through the upper basin for 2.5 miles, Thunderbolt Pass will be reached (approximately 12,000 feet).

At the top of the ridge, you will need to traverse down to the saddle below Thunderbolt's northeast ridge. You will see a pair of chutes in front of you. Take the more direct path to the southernmost chute. Following the chute takes you to the notch between Thunderbolt and Starlight. During the early season you can stay on the snow in the chute, but later in the season the best route will be to stay on the rocks (Class 3/4) on the sides. The loose footing left after the snow has melted can be challenging to climb.

Once you reach the notch that separates the two peaks, you will work up through the Class 3 slabs toward the summit. Traverse the right side of the ridge and around the corner of a headwall. Negotiating the corner requires some very exposed Class 4 moves to gain the steep blocks that take you to a flat area where you can catch your breath. Continue south along the ridge passing Thunderbolt Peak's summit block toward Starlight Peak.

After reaching the notch between Thunderbolt and Starlight Peak via the northeast ridge route described above, you have two distinct route options. Maintaining the ridge crest to Starlight is one. You can also move southwest of the ridge and traverse until the northwest face of Starlight is met. Keep your eyes on the spire to make sure to stay on route.

Passing the summit block of Starlight Peak, only a few hundred meters separates you from the summit of North Palisade. The traverse between the two will be Class 4/5 almost the entire way.

From Starlight, hike south down the ridge. You will have to negotiate some large boulders in order to reach the ridge and then a couple of very exposed moves to reach better terrain. Maintain a route on the south side of the ridge and saddle while the travel is easy. Once the route becomes challenging and a gap in the ridge is reached, cross to the north side of the ridge and descend to the west to a point where the gap can be crossed and travel to the east can resume.

Climb up to the platform on the east side. Skilled climbers can use a rope to swing to this platform, instead of using the Class 4/5 traverse, to gain the east side of the gap. Continue up the ridgeline to a chimney just below North Palisade's summit. Turn west and climb through the blocks to reach the summit. Once the summit has been gained, you can either retrace your route back north to Bishop Pass or continue on to Polemonium Peak to the south.

Hiking Information

Closest Outfitters

Big Willi Mountaineering Company, 120 S. Main St., Ste. 13 and 14, Lone Pine, CA 93545; (760) 878-2849; https://bigwillimc.com

Stop in for last-minute supplies and ask Blair about his favorite places to explore in the Sierras. If you are driving north on US 395 from picking up your permit, Big Willi is located just past the stoplight in Lone Pine.

Carroll's Market, 136 S. Main St., Big Pine, CA 93513

Great Pre- or Post-Mountain Spots

Copper Top BBQ, 310 S. Main St., Big Pine, CA 93513; (760) 970-5577; www.coppertopbbq.com

Voted the "Best Barbeque" in the country in 2015, this roadside take-out stand has become a food destination for folks across the country. Huge fan of the tri-tip after a few days in the mountains.

Aberdeen Restaurant, 150 Tinemaha Rd., Independence, CA 93526; (760) 938-2663; www.aberdeenresort.com

Shuttle Service

East Side Shuttle Service, Independence, CA; (760) 878-8047; paul@inyopro.com; ww.eastsidesierrashuttle.com

12 Polemonium Peak

Elevation: 14,100 feet, 8th highest
Start: North Fork Big Pine Creek Trailhead
(Glacier Lodge)
Distance: 25 miles round-trip
Primary route: North Fork Big Pine Creek
Trailhead to Glacier Trail to traverse from North
Palisade
Elevation gain: 6,300 feet
Hiking time: 12 to 18 hours
Difficulty: Class 1, Class 4/5
Trail surface: Dirt trail leading to talus, glacier
travel, high ridgeline exposure
Trailhead elevation: 7,800 feet
Camping: Designated camping at Glacier Lodge
campground, dispersed camping along trail

Fees: None
Permit: Yes
Best seasons: Late spring, summer, and fall;
technical winter climb
Maps: Tom Harrison The Palisades, Bishop
Pass North Lake–South Lake Loop; USGS North
Palisade
Nearest town: Big Pine, CA
Trail contact: White Mountain Ranger Station,
798 N. Main St., Bishop, CA 93514; (619)
873-2500
First ascent: July 24, 1903, Joseph LeConte,
James Moffitt, James Hutchinson, and Robert
Pike

Finding the trailhead: From the corner of US 395 and Crocker Avenue in Big Pine, head west
toward the mountains and Glacier Lodge. Crocker Avenue becomes Glacier Lodge Road just
outside of town. Stay on Glacier Lodge Road for 11 miles until you arrive at the trailhead parking
area. GPS: 37.07000°N / 118.4692°W

The Hike

From the parking area, head west onto the trail. There will be some cabins on the
right above you. Cross the bridge over the North Fork and follow this well-used trail
to a junction that offers the "upper trail" option. Your choice here is easy. You can take
the shorter and steeper upper trail or stay in the valley on the lower one. They will
end up in the exact same spot 2 miles up the trail. The lower trail follows an access
road, while the upper route is a rocky singletrack. When the two converge, the trail
starts to switchback toward Second Falls and will stay to the right of the tumbling
North Fork. While this is a very photogenic part of the trail, do not wander too close
to the water while capturing the moment.

About a mile later you will pass the ranger's cabin on the left side of the trail. The
North Fork flows gently by the covered porch of the cabin, providing a shaded and
sheltered spot to catch your breath or escape the weather. Be mindful that this is an
active bear area. Please read the section in the introduction that details how to handle
your food stores and face-to-face encounters with black bears in the Sierras. It is not
uncommon to see scratch marks in trees.

Between the cabin and First Lake, the travel will be smooth and easy. The smooth
dirt trail only gains 2,000 feet over these 6 miles as it meanders through the woods.

The North Fork will almost always be in sight on this section, which means that a fresh water source will be readily available. It would be smart to filter or purify any water at this stage, since the animal and human traffic can be high. On-trail left, Mount Alice and Temple Crag will come into view between the trees.

The mountain lakes that you will encounter are numbered like the waterfalls: First, Second, Third, and so on. This makes it easy to stay in your map and know exactly where you are. The trail junctions are also clearly marked with directional signs to keep you on route. Those looking to camp will find sites with both protection and incredible views along the shorelines. The first three lakes all sit at around 10,000 feet in elevation and are less than 2 miles apart. There are some incredible sites around each lake. In addition to the lakes, there are several small streams and springs along the trail for water.

Just past Third Lake the trail steepens and switchbacks for a period before the Glacier Trail junction. You will want to choose the Glacier Trail heading to the left. This trail may seem less maintained and slightly overgrown compared to the North Fork Trail to this point, a result of lower levels of foot traffic. The trail drops down ever so slightly in elevation as it heads back into the trees and into a marshy meadow. Stay on the rock walkway through this area to help reduce soil erosion and damage.

The tree line will slowly give way as the trail becomes rocky and somewhat loose. You will only need a mile on the Glacier Trail to enter into the green space that comprises Sam Mack Meadow. Below Sam Mack Lake the meadow features a gently rolling stream (unless you are there during early season when the snow is melting) cutting right down the middle. The trail crosses the stream via boulders left by glacial erosion. If you camp here, be mindful of the mosquitoes!

After crossing the stream, the trail climbs steeply up the cliff to the ridge to the southeast in front of you. Expect the footing to be loose in places as you traverse around the cliff. Once you come around the corner, all five summits come into view for the first time. Climbing up and over a ridge, the trail will eventually disappear as the glacial moraine begins to dominate the land. Traverse the moraine east toward the northwest ridge of Mount Gayley until it combines with the Palisade Glacier's terminal moraine. The talus field can be crossed easily during early season, but when the snow has melted, it becomes challenging both physically and mentally. You will be able to see the prominent North Couloir and your route to the ridgeline.

Make your way up the 1,000 feet through the couloir. Expect to encounter snow and ice during all seasons. Having the snow cover will aid in the crossing of talus but may require ice tools to safely navigate. Stay to the left side as you approach the ridgeline. Expect this section to take up to two hours to complete.

From the approach from the Palisade Glacier below to the final summit block, Thunderbolt Peak requires the most skill and subjects the climber to the most exposure of any of the California fourteeners.

At the top of the ridge, you will need to traverse down to the saddle below Thunderbolt's northeast ridge. You will see a pair of chutes in front of you. Take the more

Reaching Polemonium Peak, nestled between Mount Sill and North Palisade, often leads to the summit of multiple fourteeners as you hike along the ridgeline.

Small patches of snow and ice can be found across the trail throughout the year. During the winter and early in the season, crampons or micro-spikes may be required to cross these areas. Later in the season one can avoid danger by stepping around them.

direct path to the southernmost chute. Following the chute takes you to the notch between Thunderbolt and Starlight. During the early season you can stay on the snow in the chute, but later in the season the best route will be to stay on the rocks (Class 3/4) on the sides. The loose footing left after the snow has melted can be challenging to climb.

Once you reach the notch that separates the two peaks, you will work up through the Class 3 slabs toward the summit. Traverse the right side of the ridge and around the corner of a headwall. Negotiating the corner requires some very exposed Class 4 moves to gain the steep blocks that take you to a flat area where you can catch your breath. Continue south along the ridge to approach Starlight Peak.

After reaching the notch between Thunderbolt and Starlight Peak via the northeast ridge route described above, you have two distinct route options. Maintaining the ridge crest to Starlight is one. You can also move southwest of the ridge and traverse until the northwest face of Starlight is met. Keep your eyes on the spire to make sure to stay on route.

A few hundred meters is all the distance between Starlight Peak and the summit of North Palisade. The traverse between the two will be Class 4/5 almost the entire way. From Starlight, hike south down the ridge. You will have to negotiate some large boulders in order to reach the ridge and then a couple of very exposed moves to reach better terrain. Maintain a route on the south side of the ridge and saddle while the travel is easy. Once the route becomes challenging and a gap in the ridge is reached, cross to the north side of the ridge and descend to the west to a point where the gap can be crossed and travel to the east can resume.

Climb up to the platform on the east side. Skilled climbers can use a rope to swing to this platform, instead of using the Class 4/5 traverse, to gain the east side of the gap. Continue up the ridgeline to a chimney just below North Palisade's summit. Turn west and climb through the blocks to reach the summit. Once the summit has been reached, traverse south along the ridge to approach Polemonium Peak.

Polemonium Peak was considered an unnamed sub-summit of North Palisade until 1985. Due to where this peak lies geographically, it is rarely climbed alone. Sitting between North Palisade and Mount Sill, the route to this peak is solid Class 4 no matter how you approach it.

Coming from North Palisade, the route is a relatively direct and semi-exposed Class 4 climb to the summit. The scramble will require using your hands to maintain safe footing. From here, you can retrace your route back to Bishop Pass. To reach Mount Sill and complete a linkup of summits, follow the ridgeline east to the summit.

Alternate Route: Bishop Pass

Finding the trailhead: Drive south out of Bishop on CA 168. Turn left (east) onto Bishop Creek Road toward South Lake for eight miles until your reach the trailhead. There are several designated campgrounds along the way; you can reserve a spot in advance through the Recreation.gov site. The trail begins at the south end of the parking area. GPS: 37.1694; -118.5660

This route starts at a higher point (9,825 feet) than the North Fork Big Pine approach 2,000 feet lower. This approach involves a more gradual elevation gain but will require some solid route-finding skills once Bishop Pass has been reached and cross-country travel begins.

South Lake will sit on your right (west) for the first few minutes until you reach a trail junction. Stay on the left trail at this point. Just over a mile down the trail, a side trail that circumnavigates Chocolate Peak will head slightly east. Should you detour down this route, it rejoins with the trail to Bishop Pass after a couple of miles. This is a very cool side trip, and the camping along the Chocolate Lakes provides great views.

To reach Bishop Pass, however, stay on the main trail and pass Long Lake on your right. Just a touch over 5 miles from the trailhead, you will reach Bishop Pass. Dusy Basin will be below you to the south/southwest. The first view of Thunderbolt Peak will be along the ridge directly south of the pass. From this point on, you will be hiking across open ground and will need to navigate your way.

Leaving the trail just below the pass, the goal will be to traverse a contour below Mount Agassiz and Mount Winchell but above the talus lining the basin. Try to maintain an elevation close to 12,000 feet as a guideline. There is a sweet spot between the talus above and the talus below as far as the energy expenditure required. Set a bearing on the saddle between Mount Winchell and Thunderbolt Peak. After picking your way through the upper basin for 2.5 miles, Thunderbolt Pass will be reached (approximately 12,000 feet).

At the top of the ridge, you will need to traverse down to the saddle below Thunderbolt's northeast ridge. You will see a pair of chutes in front of you. Take the more direct path to the southernmost chute. Following the chute takes you to the notch between Thunderbolt and Starlight. During the early season you can stay on the snow in the chute, but later in the season the best route will be to stay on the rocks (Class 3/4) on the sides. The loose footing left after the snow has melted can be challenging to climb.

Once you reach the notch that separates the two peaks, you will work up through the Class 3 slabs toward the summit. Traverse the right side of the ridge and around the corner of a headwall. Negotiating the corner requires some very exposed Class 4 moves to gain the steep blocks that take you to a flat area where you can catch your breath. Continue south along the ridge passing Thunderbolt Peak's summit block toward Starlight Peak.

After reaching the notch between Thunderbolt and Starlight Peak via the northeast ridge route described above, you have two distinct route options. Maintaining the ridge crest to Starlight is one. You can also move southwest of the ridge and traverse until the northwest face of Starlight is met. Keep your eyes on the spire to make sure to stay on route.

A few hundred meters is all the distance between Starlight Peak and the summit of North Palisade. The traverse between the two will be Class 4/5 almost the entire way. From Starlight, hike south down the ridge. You will have to negotiate some large boulders in order to reach the ridge and then a couple of very exposed moves to reach better terrain. Maintain a route on the south side of the ridge and saddle while the travel is easy. Once the route becomes challenging and a gap in the ridge is reached, cross to the north side of the ridge and descend to the west to a point where the gap can be crossed and travel to the east can resume.

Climb up to the platform on the east side. Skilled climbers can use a rope to swing to this platform, instead of using the Class 4/5 traverse, to gain the east side of the gap. Continue up the ridgeline to a chimney just below North Palisade's summit. Turn west and climb through the blocks to reach the summit. Once the summit has been reached, traverse south along the ridge to approach Polemonium Peak.

Polemonium Peak was considered an unnamed sub-summit of North Palisade until 1985. Due to where this peak lies geographically, it is rarely climbed alone. Sitting between North Palisade and Mount Sill, the route to this peak is solid Class 4 no matter how you approach it.

Coming from North Palisade, the route is a relatively direct and semi-exposed Class 4 climb to the summit. The scramble will require using your hands to maintain safe footing. From here, you can retrace your route back to Bishop Pass. To reach Mount Sill and complete a linkup of summits, follow the ridgeline east to the summit.

Hiking Information

Closest Outfitters

Big Willi Mountaineering Company, 120 S. Main St., Ste. 13 and 14, Lone Pine, CA 93545; (760) 878-2849; https://bigwillimc.com

Stop in for last-minute supplies and ask Blair about his favorite places to explore in the Sierras. If you are driving north on US 395 from picking up your permit, Big Willi is located just past the stoplight in Lone Pine.

Carroll's Market, 136 S. Main St., Big Pine, CA 93513

Great Pre- or Post-Mountain Spots

Copper Top BBQ, 310 S. Main St., Big Pine, CA 93513; (760) 970-5577; www .coppertopbbq.com

Voted the "Best Barbeque" in the country in 2015, this roadside take-out stand has become a food destination for folks across the country. Huge fan of the tri-tip after a few days in the mountains.

Aberdeen Restaurant, 150 Tinemaha Rd., Independence, CA 93526; (760) 938-2663; www.aberdeenresort.com

Shuttle Service

East Side Shuttle Service, Independence, CA; (760) 878-8047; paul@inyopro .com; ww.eastsidesierrashuttle.com

13 Mount Sill

Elevation: 14,153 feet, 7th highest
Start: North Fork Big Pine Creek Trailhead (Glacier Lodge)
Distance: 26 miles round-trip
Primary route: North Fork Big Pine Creek Trailhead to Glacier Trail to North Couloir to traverse from Polemonium Peak
Elevation gain: 6,353 feet
Hiking time: 12 to 18 hours
Difficulty: Class 1, Class 4/5
Trail surface: Dirt trail leading to talus, glacier travel, high ridgeline exposure
Trailhead elevation: 7,800 feet
Camping: Designated camping at Glacier Lodge campground, dispersed camping along trail

Fees: None
Permit: Yes
Best seasons: Late spring, summer, and early fall; technical winter climb
Maps: Tom Harrison The Palisades, Bishop Pass North Lake–South Lake Loop; USGS North Palisade
Nearest town: Big Pine, CA
Trail contact: White Mountain Ranger Station, 798 N. Main St., Bishop, CA 93514; (619) 873-2500
First ascent: July 24, 1903, Joseph LeConte, James Moffitt, James Hutchinson, and Robert Pike

Finding the trailhead: From the corner of US 395 and Crocker Avenue in Big Pine, head west toward the mountains and Glacier Lodge. Crocker Avenue becomes Glacier Lodge Road just outside of town. Stay on Glacier Lodge Road for 11 miles until you arrive at the trailhead parking area. GPS: 37.07000°N / 118.4692°W

The Hike

From the parking area, head west onto the trail. There will be some cabins on the right above you. Cross the bridge over the North Fork and follow this well-used trail to a junction that offers the "upper trail" option. Your choice here is easy. You can take the shorter and steeper upper trail or stay in the valley on the lower one. They will end up in the exact same spot 2 miles up the trail. The lower trail follows an access road, while the upper route is a rocky singletrack. When the two converge, the trail starts to switchback toward Second Falls and will stay to the right of the tumbling North Fork. While this is a very photogenic part of the trail, do not wander too close to the water while capturing the moment.

About a mile later you will pass the ranger's cabin on the left side of the trail. The North Fork flows gently by the covered porch of the cabin, providing a shaded and sheltered spot to catch your breath or escape the weather. Be mindful that this is an active bear area. Please read the section in the introduction that details how to handle your food stores and face-to-face encounters with black bears in the Sierras. It is not uncommon to see scratch marks in trees.

Between the cabin and First Lake, the travel will be smooth and easy. The smooth dirt trail only gains 2,000 feet over these 6 miles as it meanders through the woods.

Whether you start the Palisades Traverse from Mount Sill (southern approach) or from Thunderbolt Peak (northern approach), the ridgelines of the Palisades Crest should not be taken lightly. The risk/reward factor is high with every step. Pay close attention to the cloud formations to the west as the day progresses. Getting caught during a thunderstorm can be deadly.

The North Fork will almost always be in sight on this section, which means that a fresh water source will be readily available. It would be smart to filter or purify any water at this stage, since the animal and human traffic can be high. On-trail left, Mount Alice and Temple Crag will come into view between the trees.

The mountain lakes that you will encounter are numbered like the waterfalls: First, Second, Third, and so on. This makes it easy to stay in your map and know exactly where you are. The trail junctions are also clearly marked with directional signs to keep you on route. Those looking to camp will find sites with both protection and incredible views along the shorelines. The first three lakes all sit at around 10,000 feet in elevation and are less than 2 miles apart. There are some incredible sites around each lake. In addition to the lakes, there are several small streams and springs along the trail for water.

Just past Third Lake the trail steepens and switchbacks for a period before the Glacier Trail junction. You will want to choose the Glacier Trail heading to the left. This trail may seem less maintained and slightly overgrown compared to the North Fork Trail to this point, a result of lower levels of foot traffic. The trail drops down ever so slightly in elevation as it heads back into the trees and into a marshy meadow. Stay on the rock walkway through this area to help reduce soil erosion and damage.

The tree line will slowly give way as the trail becomes rocky and somewhat loose. You will only need a mile on the Glacier Trail to enter into the green space that comprises Sam Mack Meadow. Below Sam Mack Lake the meadow features a gently rolling stream (unless you are there during early season when the snow is melting) cutting right down the middle. The trail crosses the stream via boulders left by glacial erosion. If you camp here, be mindful of the mosquitoes!

After crossing the stream, the trail climbs steeply up the cliff to the ridge to the southeast in front of you. Expect the footing to be loose in places as you traverse around the cliff. Once you come around the corner, all five summits come into view for the first time. Climbing up and over a ridge, the trail will eventually disappear as the glacial moraine begins to dominate the land. Traverse the moraine east toward the northwest ridge of Mount Gayley until it combines with the Palisade Glacier's terminal moraine. The talus field can be crossed easily during early season, but when the snow has melted, it becomes challenging both physically and mentally. You will be able to see the prominent North Couloir and your route to the ridgeline.

Make your way up the 1,000 feet through the couloir. Expect to encounter snow and ice during all seasons. Having the snow cover will aid in the crossing of talus but may require ice tools to safely navigate. Stay to the left side as you approach the ridgeline. Expect this section to take up to two hours to complete.

From the approach from the Palisade Glacier below to the final summit block, Thunderbolt Peak requires the most skill and subjects the climber to the most exposure of any of the California fourteeners.

At the top of the ridge, you will need to traverse down to the saddle below Thunderbolt's northeast ridge. You will see a pair of chutes in front of you. Take the more direct path to the southernmost chute. Following the chute takes you to the notch between Thunderbolt and Starlight. During the early season you can stay on the snow in the chute, but later in the season the best route will be to stay on the rocks (Class 3/4) on the sides. The loose footing left after the snow has melted can be challenging to climb.

Once you reach the notch that separates the two peaks, you will work up through the Class 3 slabs toward the summit. Traverse the right side of the ridge and around the corner of a headwall. Negotiating the corner requires some very exposed Class 4 moves to gain the steep blocks that take you to a flat area that you can catch your breath at. Continue south along the ridge to approach Starlight Peak.

After reaching the notch between Thunderbolt and Starlight Peak via the northeast ridge route described above, you have two distinct route options. Maintaining the ridge crest to Starlight is one. You can also move southwest of the ridge and traverse until the northwest face of Starlight is met. Keep your eyes on the spire to make sure to stay on route.

The North Couloir's (Class 4) approach up the North Fork Big Pine Creek Trail requires a higher skill set than approaching Mount Sill from the East Couloir (Class 3). The more difficult route has been chosen for this book because it shares a common approach with the neighboring fourteeners and, from an efficiency standpoint, makes sense.

Alternate Route: Bishop Pass

Finding the trailhead: Drive south out of Bishop on CA 168. Turn left (east) onto Bishop Creek Road toward South Lake for 8 miles until you reach the trailhead. There are several designated campgrounds along the way; you can reserve a spot in advance through the Recreation.gov site. The trail begins at the south end of the parking area. GPS: 37.1694; -118.5660

This route starts at a higher point (9,825 feet) than the North Fork Big Pine approach 2,000 feet lower. This approach involves a more gradual elevation gain but will require some solid route-finding skills once Bishop Pass has been reached and cross-country travel begins.

South Lake will sit on your right (west) for the first few minutes until you reach a trail junction. Stay on the left trail at this point. Just over a mile down the trail, a side trail that circumnavigates Chocolate Peak will head slightly east. Should you detour down this route, it rejoins with the trail to Bishop Pass after a couple of miles. This is a very cool side trip, and the camping along the Chocolate Lakes provides great views.

To reach Bishop Pass, however, stay on the main trail and pass Long Lake on your right. Just a touch over 5 miles from the trailhead, you will reach Bishop Pass. Dusy Basin will be below you to the south/southwest. The first view of Thunderbolt Peak will be along the ridge directly south of the pass. From this point on, you will be hiking across open ground and will need to navigate your way.

Leaving the trail just below the pass, the goal will be to traverse a contour below Mount Agassiz and Mount Winchell but above the talus lining the basin. Try to maintain an elevation close to 12,000 feet as a guideline. There is a sweet spot between the talus above and the talus below as far as the energy expenditure required. Set a bearing on the saddle between Mount Winchell and Thunderbolt Peak. After picking your way through the upper basin for 2.5 miles, Thunderbolt Pass will be reached (approximately 12,000 feet).

At the top of the ridge, you will need to traverse down to the saddle below Thunderbolt's northeast ridge. You will see a pair of chutes in front of you. Take the more direct path to the southernmost chute. Following the chute takes you to the notch between Thunderbolt and Starlight. During the early season you can stay on the snow in the chute, but later in the season the best route will be to stay on the rocks (Class 3/4) on the sides. The loose footing left after the snow has melted can be challenging to climb.

Once you reach the notch that separates the two peaks, you will work up through the Class 3 slabs toward the summit. Traverse the right side of the ridge and around the corner of a headwall. Negotiating the corner requires some very exposed Class 4 moves to gain the steep blocks that take you to a flat area that you can catch your breath at. Traverse around Thunderbolt Peak's summit block south toward Starlight Peak.

After reaching the notch between Thunderbolt and Starlight Peak via the northeast ridge route described above, you have two distinct route options. Maintaining the

Hidden tarns can provide water access during your hike. Make sure to filter and purify any water used for drinking and cooking to avoid ingesting bacteria that may make you ill.

ridge crest to Starlight is one. You can also move southwest of the ridge and traverse until the northwest face of Starlight is met. Keep your eyes on the spire to make sure to stay on route.

A few hundred meters is all the distance between Starlight Peak and the summit of North Palisade. The traverse between the two will be Class 4/5 almost the entire way. From Starlight, hike south down the ridge. You will have to negotiate some large boulders in order to reach the ridge and then a couple of very exposed moves to reach better terrain. Maintain a route on the south side of the ridge and saddle while the travel is easy. Once the route becomes challenging and a gap in the ridge is reached, cross to the north side of the ridge and descend to the west to a point where the gap can be crossed and travel to the east can resume.

Climb up to the platform on the east side. Skilled climbers can use a rope to swing to this platform, instead of using the Class 4/5 traverse, to gain the east side of the gap. Continue up the ridgeline to a chimney just below North Palisade's summit. Turn west and climb through the blocks to reach the summit. Once the summit has been reached, traverse south along the ridge to approach Polemonium Peak.

Polemonium Peak was considered an unnamed sub-summit of North Palisade until 1985. Due to where this peak lies geographically, it is rarely climbed alone. Sitting between North Palisade and Mount Sill, the route to this peak is solid Class 4 no matter how you approach it.

Coming from North Palisade, the route is a relatively direct and semi-exposed Class 4 climb to Polemonium's summit. The scramble will require using your hands to maintain safe footing. To reach Mount Sill and complete a linkup of summits, follow the ridgeline east to the summit.

From Polemonium Peak, continue to hike south/southeast along the ridgeline to the summit of Mount Sill. Making this traverse will take you across some Class 3 terrain.

Instead of retracing your steps to return to Bishop Pass from Mount Sill, use the following route. Continue to the saddle between Mount Sill and Mount Gayley. Downclimb the slabs through the East Couloir to reach the Palisade Glacier basin below. Snow and ice may be encountered in the chute, but there should be solid footing available.

Once you have reached the basin, traverse the moraine east toward the northwest ridge of Mount Gayley until it combines with the Palisade Glacier's terminal moraine. You will be able to see the prominent North Couloir and your route to the ridgeline.

Make your way up the 1,000 feet through the couloir. Expect to encounter snow and ice during all seasons. Having the snow cover will aid in the crossing of talus but may require ice tools to safely navigate. Stay to the left side as you approach the ridgeline. Expect this section to take up to two hours to complete.

Once on top of Thunderbolt Pass, descend on the west side back into Dusy Basin and travel through the talus back to the trail at Bishop Pass and ultimately the trailhead.

Hiking Information

Closest Outfitters

Big Willi Mountaineering Company, 120 S. Main St., Ste. 13 and 14, Lone Pine, CA 93545; (760) 878-2849; https://bigwillimc.com

Stop in for last-minute supplies and ask Blair about his favorite places to explore in the Sierras. If you are driving north on US 395 from picking up your permit, Big Willi is located just past the stoplight in Lone Pine.

Carroll's Market, 136 S. Main St., Big Pine, CA 93513

Great Pre- or Post-Mountain Spots

Copper Top BBQ, 310 S. Main St., Big Pine, CA 93513; (760) 970-5577; www .coppertopbbq.com

Voted the "Best Barbeque" in the country in 2015, this roadside take-out stand has become a food destination for folks across the country. Huge fan of the tri-tip after a few days in the mountains.

Aberdeen Restaurant, 150 Tinemaha Rd., Independence, CA 93526; (760) 938-2663; www.aberdeenresort.com

Shuttle Service

East Side Shuttle Service, Independence, CA; (760) 878-8047; paul@inyopro .com; www.eastsidesierrashuttle.com

14 White Mountain

Elevation: 14,252, 3rd highest
Start: Barcroft Research Facility access road
Distance: 14 miles round-trip
Primary route: South Slope
Elevation gain: 2,246 feet
Hiking time: 7 to 10 hours
Difficulty: Class 1
Trail surface: Gravel road leading to gravel trail
Trailhead elevation: 12,000 feet

Camping: Dispersed camping at trailhead parking area
Fees: None
Permit: Not required
Best seasons: Summer and fall
Map: USGS White Mountain
Nearest town: Big Pine, CA
Trail contact: White Mountain Ranger District, 798 N. Main St., Bishop, CA 93514; (760) 873-2500
First ascent: Aboriginal Tribes, around 600 AD

Finding the trailhead: Just north of Big Pine, turn east on CA 168. In 13 miles, turn left (north) onto White Mountain Road. At 23 miles, the Ancient Bristlecone Pine Forest Visitor Center will be on the right; proceed through the gate. At 32.5 miles, turn right (east) to Crooked Creek Station. At 40 miles, arrive at the parking area below the Barcroft Research Facility. GPS: 37.63440°N / 118.25701°W

The Hike

While White Mountain may not be the most technical fourteener around, as you will literally hike from the trailhead to the summit on an access road, do not underestimate this mountain just because the route is easy to follow. We rank this the easiest of the California fourteeners to summit based on the Class 1 route, but you will still be climbing the third-tallest peak in the state.

At 14,246 feet, the air is rare and the vistas are expansive. Located within Inyo National Forest, this mountain is one of our favorites for year-round climbing. Most years from May through mid-October the trail is clear and dry, requiring only your boots or shoes for traction. During the winter months you can expect to find areas of 2 to 4 feet of snow and patches of ice along the route. Snowshoes and crampons become necessary in these conditions. You do not need a permit to hike or climb this mountain.

On the eastern border of the Owens Valley, White Mountain's flora and fauna are vastly different from the Sierra's, contributing to a completely different feel from the other mountains. The easiest access to the trailhead is via CA 168 out of Big Pine and White Mountain Road. Along the way you pass the Sierra Viewpoint's view of the Sierras to the west and the Ancient Bristlecone Pine Forest Visitor Center at Schulman Grove. Within the grove you will find the oldest bristlecone pines in the world. Many of them are older than 4,000 years and continue to flourish and grow.

With its straightforward hike and minimal need for route-finding, White Mountain is a great "starter" fourteener for any hiker.

Once you pass the visitor center, the road surface changes from pavement to dirt. While a high-clearance four-wheel-drive vehicle makes the trip more comfortable, with care and patience you can reach the trailhead in almost any car. The road is wide enough for cars to pass with care. Just to be safe, throw a can or two of tire sealant in the trunk, since you will be a long way from a tow truck. The road will be rough and rocky in places, so be mindful of the changing conditions. There is a defined parking area at the gate—please leave your vehicle in the marked area to prevent damage to the plant life. You will find a pit toilet along with a trash can near the parking area.

Tucked high in the White Mountains, the Ancient Bristlecone Pine Forest is home to some of the oldest living trees in the world. Visiting the forest is a great way to acclimatize on the way to the top of White Mountain.

Unless you have acclimated to the elevation prior to arriving, it would be wise to camp for the night. There are several primitive sites close to the parking area. If you set up your tent to the east of the gate in the drainage, please be mindful of the weather conditions, as rain could wash your gear down the mountain. Since the drive in on White Mountain Road can take 2 to 4 hours to complete, many people will arrive in the mid- to late-afternoon so they can start hiking early the following day. Chances

On the drive from Big Pine to the trailhead, the Ancient Bristlecone Pine Forest provides an educational side trip. Home to the oldest non-clonal organisms on the planet, these trees have withstood Mother Nature's test time for thousands of years. A walk through the forest serves as a reminder of how young humans really are.

are you will be sharing the dispersed camping area and the trail with others. Dispersed camping is not permitted in the Bristlecone Pine Forest. Spending the night at 12,000 feet before you summit will make the trip more enjoyable. Set up camp and then shake out the legs by hiking up to the Barcroft Research Facility at 12,470 feet.

Practice the "Leave No Trace" principles. Pack out what you take in with you. The backcountry that is home to the fourteeners will be pristine when you enter and should remain the same as you leave. Stay on designated trails where they are available. When traveling cross-country, be mindful of your impact on the land you step on. White Mountain's topography makes it difficult to bury human waste in "catholes." Please take WAG bags to carry out any solid human waste. We also suggest packing biodegradable wipes. You can deposit any waste or trash items in the receptacle at the trailhead.

The trailhead sits well above the tree line at 12,000 feet, which means the entire route faces total exposure to the elements. With just over 2,000 feet of elevation to gain from the parking area to the summit, it can be tempting to make a speedy ascent to the top. The 14-mile round-trip hike can prove deceiving in its difficulty, however. The route follows the access road to the summit. What this mountain may lack in technical difficulty, it makes up for in other ways. The trail is very straightforward all the way to the summit. You may even find you have phone service at certain points. Even though the route is very distinct, make sure that someone knows when you left camp and when you plan to return. Sharing your itinerary allows for good communication with the authorities in case of an emergency.

A short 2 miles after leaving the trailhead, you will reach the Barcroft facility. The trail stays to the right and passes some aromatic sheep pens. Originally constructed in 1951 to study the effects of high altitude on pilots for the military and currently maintained by the University of California system, researchers at this facility have studied physiology, astronomy, geology, and zoology. Located at 12,470 feet, Barcroft can house up to 20 researchers at a time. Its unique geographic location, away from light pollution and human contamination, allows controlled and unobstructed studies. Do not plan on sheltering or using the facilities at Barcroft, as they are reserved for the research staff.

Stay along the road south of the buildings and the livestock pens to find the trail. Do not be surprised if this trail looks surprisingly like an access road. It is. The road makes route-finding easy and provides access to Summit Lab on top of White Mountain.

Keep your eyes on the weather to the west as you climb, since the normal pattern moves west to east. It is common for rain to fall in the afternoons. If you see lightning in the distance, turn around and go back to camp. Lightning is very unpredictable and life-threatening. You do not want to be caught on the ridgeline in an electrical storm. Remember, there is absolutely no shelter on this trail.

Above the observatory, you will come across a random White Mountain sign to the side of the trail. At 13,000 feet, and the summit in sight, the trail drops down a very rocky section and then starts a series of long switchbacks to the summit. It may

Built in the 1960s, the foundation of the observatory stands as a reminder of the research that has been conducted in this region. The observatory is no longer used for research. Currently, the University of California's White Mountain Research Center researches the effects of altitude on humans and animals.

Starting just after sunrise, Nick Niforos of Albuquerque, New Mexico, makes his way up the trail to White Mountain. Using trekking poles, like these from Mons Peak IX, helps maintain balance and distribute the weight of your pack over your center of mass, making the hike more comfortable.

be tempting, especially on the way down, to cut across the switchbacks. Please stay on the designated trail. From the base of White Mountain to the summit you will gain about 1,500 feet in just around a mile, making the final push the most physically demanding section.

Rounding the final turn and taking a few more steps provides a view that encompasses Nevada to the east and the Owens Valley and the Sierras to the west. Looking north and south, the entire White Mountain Range lies before you. Death Valley, home to the lowest elevation point in North America, lies to the southeast. Make sure to sign the summit book and take some pictures before you start down the trail!

Since the mountain is accessible year-round, the type and amount of gear you will need will vary. Once you leave the trailhead, you will be looking at a 7- to 10-hour trip up and back. Your pack should, at a minimum, include a first-aid kit, a waterproof jacket, sunscreen, water, food, camera, and sunglasses. I always have a satellite tracking device in an easy-to-reach place on my pack. Not only will this allow me to send an SOS message in the event of an emergency, but it also allows my progress to be tracked so people know where I am in relation to my itinerary.

It can be tempting to skimp on the amount of water you carry. Water weighs more than almost everything in your pack combined, but it is vital to your body performing at its best during the climb. Access to water sources once you turn onto White Mountain Road is limited at best. You may find some snow that can be melted during your climb, but count on carrying water for the entire hike. Since the trailhead is above the tree line, shade and shelter on the trail is even more limited. Once you hike past the research facility and the old observatory, the only shelter options will be behind a pile of rocks along the side of the trail. A brimmed hat, sunscreen, and long sleeves are all suggested for your protection. Wind gusts on the summit have been recorded above gale force. While the trail/road is lightly maintained, the footing will be rocky and uneven in sections.

It is easy to forget to drink and eat while at altitude. You will need nourishment over the course of the climb even though you may not feel like eating. Working at elevation can have that effect. Hydration is equally important, as your muscles rely on water levels to perform at their peak. Set an alarm to remind you every 20 to 30 minutes to eat and drink, and you'll have a more enjoyable experience.

Due to the lack of shelter and shade on the route to the summit, you will be exposed to the elements from trailhead to summit and back. Understanding each of the challenges the elements present and being proactive in your preparation will make your time on every climb more enjoyable. After spending the night camped at the trailhead, gear up for a 4- to 5-hour hike to the top. Coming back down should take a little less time. Leaving before sunrise will limit your sun exposure, but plan on there being a chill in the air. It is a general rule to start your climb a little bit cold. As you progress up the mountain, your body will generate heat and you may find you need to stop to remove layers.

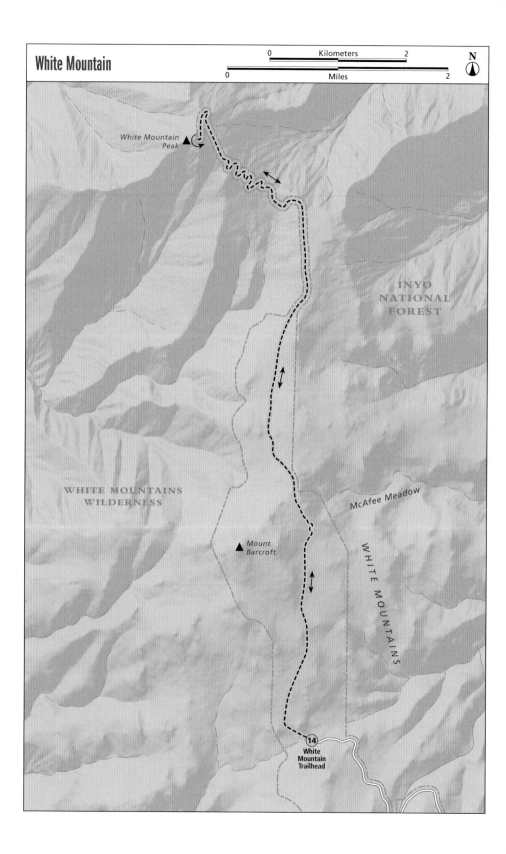

Kilometers

0   2

Miles

0   2

N

White Mountain Peak ▲

INYO NATIONAL FOREST

WHITE MOUNTAINS WILDERNESS

McAfee Meadow

▲ Mount Barcroft

WHITE MOUNTAINS

14
White Mountain Trailhead

At the true summit of each of the fourteeners, you will find a weatherproof box that houses the summit register. Climbers reaching the summit can sign the book as a record of their success. Often there will be small signs in the box with the name of the mountain and the elevation to complete your summit selfie.

The sun's rays are more powerful the higher in elevation you climb. Even on colder days, your skin can be sunburned climbing a fourteener. To protect your body, long sleeves and pants are suggested. Wear synthetic fiber products that will be breathable and lightweight. Stay away from jeans and cotton shirts, as they will retain moisture and potentially chafe. If you choose to wear shorts and short sleeves, remember to apply sunscreen and reapply it often. Do not forget your ears, nose, and the back of your neck! A brimmed hat will add another layer of sun protection to those sensitive areas.

Hiking Information

Closest Outfitters

Big Willi Mountaineering Company, 120 S. Main St., Ste. 13 and 14, Lone Pine, CA 93545; (760) 878-2849; https://bigwillimc.com

Stop in for last-minute supplies and ask Blair about his favorite places to explore in the Sierras. If you are driving north on US 395, Big Willi is located just past the stoplight in Lone Pine.

Carroll's Market, 136 S. Main St., Big Pine, CA 93513

Great Pre- or Post-Mountain Spots

Copper Top BBQ, 310 S. Main St., Big Pine, CA 93513; (760) 970-5577; www.coppertopbbq.com

Voted the "Best Barbeque" in the country in 2015, this roadside take-out stand has become a food destination for folks across the country. Huge fan of the tri-tip after a few days in the mountains.

Aberdeen Restaurant, 150 Tinemaha Rd., Independence, CA 93526; (760) 938-2663; www.aberdeenresort.com

Shuttle Service

East Side Shuttle Service, Independence, CA; (760) 878-8047; paul@inyopro.com; www.eastsidesierrashuttle.com

15 Mount Shasta

Elevation: 14,162 feet, 6th highest
Start: Bunny Flat Trailhead
Distance: 22 miles round-trip
Primary route: Bunny Flat Trailhead to Avalanche Gulch
Elevation gain: 6,862 feet
Hiking time: 12 to 18 hours
Difficulty: Class 1, Class 3 (snow and ice)
Trail surface: Dirt trail leading to talus, glacier travel
Trailhead elevation: 7,300 feet
Camping: Designated camping at Bunny Flat Trailhead, dispersed camping at Helen Lake

Fees: None
Permit: Yes
Best seasons: Late spring, summer, and early fall; technical winter climb
Maps: Tom Harrison Maps, Mount Shasta; Wilderness Press, Mt. Shasta Wilderness
Nearest town: Mount Shasta, CA
Trail contact: US Forest Service, Shasta-Trinity National Forest, 3644 Avtech Parkway Redding, CA 96002; (530) 226-2500
First ascent: 1854, E.D. Pearce

Finding the trailhead: From the intersection of Lake Street and Mount Shasta Boulevard in Mount Shasta, turn right (northeast) onto Lake Street. Bear to the left as Lake Street becomes Everitt Memorial Highway. At 11.5 miles, arrive at the Bunny Flat Trailhead parking area. GPS: 41.41000°N / 122.195°W

The Hike

Legend has it that the dormant volcano we know as Mount Shasta holds mystical powers within her belly. Legend also says that the second-most-popular fourteener in California is home to a special energy source that rejuvenates and binds our bodies, minds, and spirits. According to some people, this volcano, which last erupted in 1786, sits over an alien city hidden deep in the earth. What we know for sure is that this volcanic mountain rises majestically over the valleys below and, for mountaineers, holds its own magic at the summit.

Partly due to the legends surrounding the mountain and partly due to the very accessible trailheads, Mount Shasta has become one of the most popular mountains not only in California but in the entire United States, with more than 26,000 people visiting annually. Mountaineers often will use Mount Shasta, with its sudden weather changes, glacier travel, and elevation, to train for taller peaks around the world.

No matter which direction you approach the town of Mount Shasta from, you will be afforded incredible views of the snowy mountain. During the late summer the snowpack will diminish, but there will always be patches of white visible, enhancing the mountain's beauty. Getting to the trailhead at Bunny Flat is a very easy drive up the lower slopes of the mountain.

After spending the night at Helen Lake, Jared Wigg celebrates reaching the summit of Mount Shasta. From Helen Lake, the next 2,000 feet of elevation will be gained by crossing glaciers, snow, and ice. Depending on the time of year, you might very well be wearing crampons from Trail Camp to the summit.

Between climbers, campers, and those evoking the mountain's legendary status, the Bunny Flat Trailhead will be active around the clock. It has a self-serve kiosk where climbing permits are filled out, along with some restrooms. Make sure to pick up a WAG bag to pack out human waste as well. The trail starts just right of the kiosk. Whether your plan is to make the summit in a day or to camp at Helen Lake at the end of day one, make sure you have your ice axe and crampons (and are comfortable using them) before you head toward the Sierra Club hut at Horse Camp just over a mile away. Be sure to stop at the hut and ask the volunteer for the latest mountain conditions.

Take advantage of the spring next to the hut to top off your water supply, as this is one of the few flowing water sources on the mountain. From the hut, you will be just over 4 miles and 6,000 feet in elevation gain from standing on the summit. Just beyond the hut is the Olberman Causeway, a stone causeway named after the original resident of the hut. Stay on the stones, as they have been placed to help reduce the effects of soil erosion. The causeway transforms into a well-defined trail that snakes through a series of talus fields. The tree line falls away once you leave the causeway, leaving you exposed to the elements. There are very few boulders large enough to provide any shade and relief from the sun. Depending on the extremity of the winter and the time of year you're climbing, do not be surprised to encounter snow on the trail below Helen Lake.

For those planning on camping, Helen Lake is the destination. While the lake will likely be covered with ice and snow, there are several defined campsites on the rocky bench that overlooks Mount Shasta below. Since Helen Lake sits well above the tree line and offers little in the form of wind or sun protection, set your tent up shortly after arriving. This will provide shelter and shade and a place to recover before attempting the summit. In early or late season and in years where the winter has been long, you may need to dig a spot in the snow for your tent. Expect to not have access to the lake for fresh water. This means you will have to melt snow to have drinking and cooking water. Melting snow can be a time-consuming process, so plan on getting the stove set up and ready well in advance. We suggest walking into the snowfield and away from the campsites to gather snow.

Pro tip: Pack a plastic or waterproof bag in your kit to carry snow back to the camping area. This will save having to make multiple trips to gather snow. As the snow melts, the debris encapsulated in it will fall to the bottom of your cooking pot. Pour off the fresh water, leaving about a quarter inch in the bottom of the pan to keep rocks and dirt from getting into your bottle.

The campsites vary in size and can accommodate up to four-person tents. Rock walls have been built to provide protection from the wind. Depending on the number of climbers camping on a given night, privacy and seclusion might be a luxury. Remember to use the WAG bag you picked up at the trailhead for human waste. There is usually a designated "toilet" area near the campsites that offers a minimal amount of privacy. Spending the night at Helen Lake offers some incredible views of world below.

If you time your trip right, you can leave Helen Lake for the summit under the light of a full moon. The full moon adds to the mysticism of the mountain, and you may find that the campgrounds near the trailhead are full of people wanting to tap into that energy. Departing camp around 3:00 a.m. should allow you to reach the summit around sunrise during the summer months. For a climber, however, the full

The Sierra Club owns and maintains this cabin and the campsites around it on the way up Mount Shasta. There is a fresh water source during warmer months just outside the cabin. Make sure to stop here and ask how the trail and snow conditions are farther up the mountain.

At Helen Lake you will find several spots perfect for pitching your tent for the night. There is a profound lack of shade and natural shelter, though. Once you arrive here, make sure to set up your tent to escape the sun's rays. You will also want to start melting snow for cooking and drinking water shortly after arriving to camp. Olya Andronova and her Mons Peak IX tent enjoyed spending the night with an incredible view.

moon means that your path up the right side of Avalanche Gulch through the snow will be illuminated.

Leaving in the predawn hours when the air is crisp and the top layer of snow is still frozen will provide solid footing. Stay to the east side, or right of the Heart, while in Avalanche Gulch. Avalanches and rockfalls generally will originate from the Red Banks (northwest) or the Heart (north) above Helen Lake. From the bottom of the Heart, locate the prominent Thumb on Sargents Ridge southeast of Red Banks and traverse the saddle between the two.

Occasionally, cracks in the ice and snow called "crevasses" will form, making travel unsafe and dangerous between the Thumb and Red Banks. In this case, the route will traverse just below the ridge and up through a chute at Red Banks. As mentioned above, always stop at the Sierra Club hut for the most up-to-date mountain and weather conditions. Changing weather conditions have caught climbers in whiteout blizzard conditions with gale-force winds on exposed sections of the mountain. The important concept to keep in mind is that the mountain will always be there and

Chris Parker negotiates his way up the Heartbreak Hill switchbacks enroute to the summit of Mount Shasta via the Avalanche Gulch route.

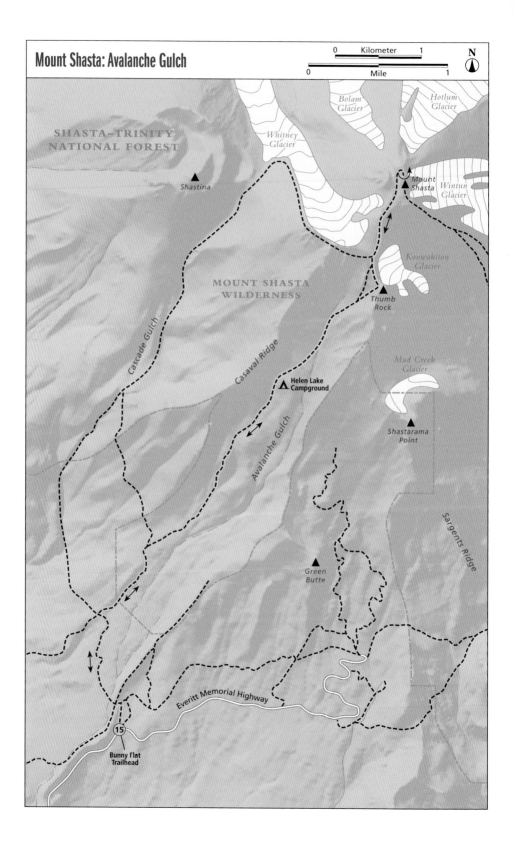

Mount Shasta: Avalanche Gulch

0   Kilometer   1

0   Mile   1

N

Bolam Glacier

Hotlum Glacier

Whitney Glacier

SHASTA–TRINITY NATIONAL FOREST

Shastina

Mount Shasta

Wintun Glacier

Konwakiton Glacier

MOUNT SHASTA WILDERNESS

Thumb Rock

Cascade Gulch

Casaval Ridge

Mud Creek Glacier

Helen Lake Campground

Shastarama Point

Avalanche Gulch

Green Butte

Sargents Ridge

Everitt Memorial Highway

15

Bunny Flat Trailhead

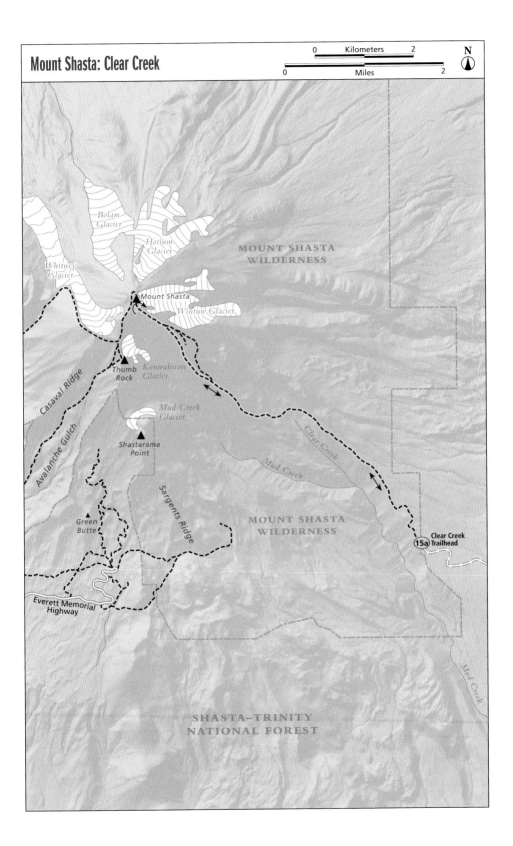

0   Kilometers   2

0   Miles   2

N

Bolam
Glacier

Hotlum
Glacier

Whitney
Glacier

MOUNT SHASTA
WILDERNESS

Wintun Glacier

Mount Shasta

Thumb
Rock

Konwakiton
Glacier

Casaval Ridge

Mud Creek
Glacier

Avalanche Gulch

Shastarama
Point

Clear Creek

Mud Creek

Sargents Ridge

Green
Butte

MOUNT SHASTA
WILDERNESS

Clear Creek
Trailhead

15a

Everett Memorial
Highway

SHASTA–TRINITY
NATIONAL FOREST

Mud Creek

Mount Shasta, according to some, sits on top of an alien community and has been the source of UFO abduction claims. The mountain is a great and powerful source of energy to others. Native tribes revered this volcanic mountain, and mountain climbers scale to her summit to test their physical and mental skills. Witnessing Shasta's shadow stretch across the valley and mountains below, it is easy to be awestruck.

> Mount Shasta is considered by the metaphysical community to be a vortex of energy and spirituality. Legends are told of people disappearing from this snowcapped volcano only to return years later with stories of a civilization under the mountain. The spiritual community often gathers on the mountain under a full moon.

attempting to summit in less-than-ideal conditions is not worth risking injury or your life for.

Once the top of Red Banks has been reached, follow the cairns to the base of Misery Hill. Often you can remove your crampons at this point, since the rocky trail surface is frequently exposed. The multiple switchbacks do little to diminish the steepness of the climb. Topping Misery Hill, you will find the summit plateau and the final push to the summit. The volcanic rock may be covered with snow and ice. The general slope is slight, so you may be able to cross this section without your crampons. The summit will be very obvious to the north. Making your way up the loose trail, you will smell and then see the sulfur hot springs, or "fumeroles," to your left. The final 100 feet of climbing will be over a loose and rocky scramble. Be mindful of other climbers, as rocks and debris may fall on those climbing below you.

The descent route simply traces your footsteps back down the mountain. As simple as this may sound, the challenge is maintaining balance and footing while downclimbing on glaciers, ice, and snow. Take your time and be mindful of the changing snow conditions. As the sun rises and works around the mountain, the top layer of snow may become soft and slushy, making the footing slick. If you have learned proper glissading technique from a professional instructor prior to your summit attempt, the level of snowpack may permit this manner of descending. Only use this technique when the conditions allow. Later in the season when much of the snow has melted, talus and boulders become exposed, posing dangers to sliding down the mountain.

The hike from Helen Lake to the trailhead will pass quickly, and the welcome shade and dirt trail once you reach the hut allow for easy travel. This mountain has many stories and legends surrounding its history. Witnessing the shadow of Mount Shasta cast over the valley to the west as the sun rises truly is a magical experience.

Alternate Route: Clear Creek Trailhead (Class 2/3)

Finding the trailhead: From McCloud, take CA 89 west. Follow the Clear Creek signs for 13.5 miles. The final 8 miles to the trailhead will be dirt. Four-wheel drive is usually not required unless heading in during early/mid-spring. The road is rough in areas, but overall a two-wheel-drive passenger vehicle can make it in without a problem. GPS: 42.37324, -122.59770

The southeast-facing Clear Creek route to the summit of Mount Shasta presents a longer but more gradual approach compared to the Avalanche Gulch route described above. Considered to be the least technical of the routes to the summit, the Clear Creek route begins shaded by fir trees at 6,390 feet. Even though this route potentially requires less technical skills than other approaches to the summit, do not venture up without proper mountaineering gear. This includes an ice axe, crampons, and a helmet for safety. The challenging aspect of the Clear Creek approach will be staying on the trail.

This route is best utilized during early season when there is slight snow or ice covering the loose rocks and talus. You can proceed almost directly up the ridgeline between the Watkins Glacier to the west and the Wintun Glacier to the east. The first 2 miles of dirt trail give way to rock at 8,100 feet. From here, without snow cover, the footing gets a little loose. A natural spring can be found near the trail just below 8,500 feet. Please be mindful of the area around the spring, as this is a fragile area. Do not camp closer than 100 feet to this water source and do your best not to trample the area while filling up your water supplies.

The steepest and most challenging section of this route comes where the ridge above the Wintun Glacier and the summit plateau meet. Snow and ice may be encountered here. Falling rock, especially shortly after the snowmelt begins, is not uncommon. Even though this approach is considered one of the easiest to the summit, dangerous conditions do exist.

Once on the summit plateau, the final push to the summit awaits. The volcanic rock may be covered with snow and ice. The general slope is slight, so you may be able to cross this section without your crampons. The summit will be very obvious to the north. Making your way up the loose trail, you will smell and then see the sulfur hot springs, or "fumeroles," to your left. The final 100 feet of climbing will be over a loose and rocky scramble. Be mindful of other climbers, as rocks and debris may fall on those climbing below you. Make your descent by retracing your footsteps back to the trailhead.

Hiking Information

Closest Outfitters

The Fifth Season, 300 N. Mount Shasta Blvd., Mount Shasta, CA 96067; (530) 926-3606; www.thefifthseason.com

Mount Shasta Super Market, 112 E. Alma St., Mount Shasta, CA 96067

Ray's Food Place, 160 Morgan Way, Mount Shasta, CA 96067

Great Pre- or Post-Mountain Spots

Yaks Mount Shasta Koffee & Eatery, 333 N. Mount Shasta Blvd., Mount Shasta, CA 96067

Cooper's Bar & Grill, 111 Morgan Way, Mount Shasta, CA 96067

Summiting the California Fourteeners:
An Author's Retrospective

I am just a regular dude. I'm not a superior athlete with mad climbing or mountaineering skills. I like to challenge and push my limits and skills. I take calculated risks, and I have been doing that since I was a kid. Which is why I found myself on a plane in 2001 going to a strange country to participate in a sport I had only watched in awe on television.

I first met Jack McBroom on a flight to New Zealand. Actually, I saw him on the plane and spent 8 hours creating the character I wanted him to be. So out of place and unsure of the unique situation I had wandered into as a competitor in the Eco-Challenge New Zealand adventure race (my first adventure race ever), playing it cool was the route I chose. After my gear became a yard sale with boxes and bags falling on the tarmac several embarrassing times, I heard Jack chuckling in my general direction. He offered a hand and pretty much made sure I made it to the next flight.

We were on separate teams that race. His was experienced and had been racing together for some time. Mine . . . well, I met my teammates for the first time as we boarded the plane in Los Angeles, so you can imagine the bond we shared. Before, during, and after the race, Jack was positive and supportive, and the more I learned about him, the more intrigued I became and a chance encounter became a friendship.

In late 2001 I moved to California for "work" and became a regular at the McBroom house during the holidays, and teamed with Jack and one of my New Zealand teammates, JD Ahern, when adventure racing season rolled around. During the Cal-Eco finals, Jack mentioned that he was going to try to set a new speed record for summiting all of the fourteeners in the state.

Being from a part of Iowa that tickles 600 feet above sea level, I did not understand the magnitude of what his goal would mean (it took me several years to really understand). A matter of days postrace (we finished sixth among some of the best teams in the world), Jack set a new "fastest known time" at 4 days, 11 hours, and 19 minutes. (Sean O'Rourke, whose book served as a guide during this project, set a new standard at 2 days, 14 hours, 3 minutes in 2012.) At the time I raised a shot of tequila to my friend, but had no idea how this feat would affect me over the next decade and a half.

My days of competing for race wins and prize money ended years ago. Competing against the clock over the same distances I ran in my youth did not hold the appeal it once did. Mostly because even though my body knew I would never come close to the times I ran postcollege, my mind was still convinced it was possible.

My focus shifted to getting back to the activities I loved as a kid. Riding my bike, running through the woods, pushing my physical and mental limits without the need of a medal at the end of the day. Reconnecting with my longtime friend Rob (as kids we used a garden hose to rappel into a local park) and meeting my training partner JT provided me outlets for pushing to my limits.

Always in the back of my mind were those damn mountains in eastern California. Could I reach each summit? And, if so, how quickly could I do it? Would it be possible to break Sean's standard and reclaim the record in the name of my friend Jack? I had not a clue as to what it would take to climb one, let alone 15, mountain over 14,000 feet.

During my adventure racing career, some peaks in that range were crossed during races, and I had taken the tram up Pike's Peak while in high school. I had spent a little time climbing indoors as well. That was the base of my experience prior to starting this project.

I knew from reading trail reports and the couple of guidebooks that were around that if I was in decent shape and took my time, several of the fourteeners could be summited without the need of technical climbing skills. But then there was the group of mountains in the Palisades that I knew would require me to work on my technique to even attempt reaching their peaks, and I would need to brush up.

This book came to fruition as a result of my desire to learn about the California fourteeners. At a trade show, I managed to corner one of the FalconGuides staff and after a lengthy and detailed conversation left with a contract to write a guidebook for them. What had I just gotten myself into?

I spent the spring and early summer preparing my body and mind for the unknown: Would I get altitude sickness? How would my body react to the challenges? Was I, at my age, pushing the limits of what I could do?

In August, I convinced my friend Nick Niforos to meet me in Las Vegas and then drive to the Sierras and attempt to get over the 14,000-foot mark. With sustained winds over 30 mph from Mount Langley to the Palisades the first couple days we planned to climb, we made the smart decision to drive up to the Reno/Tahoe area and acclimate until the wind died down.

Three days later we found our way to the White Mountain trailhead. I thought the smart plan would be to hit the easier mountains first. Heading up the trail before sunrise, we made good time past Barcroft and the observatory. I made my first rookie mistake (there would be many more to come) by recognizing that even though the air temperature seemed cool, I was more exposed to the sun's rays and neglected to put on sunscreen. Here's a tip: Apply sunscreen early and often!

The feeling upon reaching that summit, even though it was just a walk up a gravel road, was incredible. My heart hadn't exploded, and I was breathing crisp mountain air. More importantly, I was one-fifteenth of the way to writing this book. Four more mountains were conquered, including Mount Whitney, on that trip, and I returned to Iowa stoked on my progress.

There are many gear outfitters between Bishop and Lone Pine, and Nick and I walked into almost all of them. Almost to a shop, the employees looked us up and down taking in the sunburned noses and either ignored us or treated us like outsiders.

*Mount Whitney and Mount Muir
seen from the Alabama Hills*

Our questions were answered with minimal words and a touch of sarcasm. I was trying to learn about these mountains and doing research for this book. I also did not reveal that I was writing a guidebook because I wanted to be treated like a regular customer.

In Lone Pine we noticed a sign on the street for Big Willi Mountaineering and walked into an enclosed courtyard leading to one of the smallest outdoor stores I have ever been in. Trying not to feel jaded based on how we had been received in other shops, we were greeted by the only employee and owner, Blair. He asked what we were up to, offered a beer, and suggested a guidebook and a really cool spot to camp on the way up Split Mountain. He was cool and willing to share information and advice with a couple of strangers. That made an impression on me.

During the fall, I made a couple more trips through Lone Pine and stopped into Blair's shop. He was still warm and welcoming, and eventually I let it slip that I was writing this book. That information didn't change how he treated me, or how he treated others who came into his store while I was there. Turns out that he and I share a mutual friend in Jack McBroom as well. I'm not telling you where to buy your gear, but if you happen to be in Lone Pine, California, at least stop in and say hello. Blair is a good dude and might even offer you a cold beverage!

To add credibility to the project, I thought that some winter climbing should be included. In order to prepare for the cold temps, I spent several December and January nights camping in the front yard. This allowed me to gauge how quickly the battery life of my SiOnyx Aurora Camera and Bivystick GPS tracker would be affected by subzero temperatures. I would hike to my office with a fully loaded Osprey backpack, testing outerwear from Terracea, Big Agnes, and Himali. I was ready to head back to the Sierras.

Unfortunately for me, the snow started to fall in the mountains above the Owens Valley. And it kept on falling. I canceled three trips between late February and April due to continuous blizzard-like conditions. Finally, in late May there was a break in the weather. The snowpack was deeper than it had been in years, but I needed to get back out and get up the mountain!

The goal was to hike up Shepards Pass to summit Mount Williamson and Mount Tyndall, then make an approach of Mount Barnard from the John Muir Trail, then return to the car. Unfortunately, just below Shepards Pass the weather closed in and a late-season storm prevented our group from a summit attempt. The weather was supposed to be clear, and the lesson here is to keep an eye on the sky and pay attention to how rapidly things can change from bluebird to life-threatening.

For many of these mountains I either had friends with me or met some very cool people along the trail and we buddied up. The experience of hiking and climbing to these amazing peaks with someone, sharing the effort and smiles with anybody really, was so much more satisfying than those summits I reached alone. Thanks to Nick, Karina, Deborah, Brittany, Ados, Oly, Chris, Jared, and Christie for the trail time.

White Mountain, Nick Niforos on the trail. More people attempt to summit Mount Whitney annually than the other California fourteeners combined. As the tallest mountain in the United States (outside of Alaska), the allure of standing on the summit brings more than 100,000 people to the trailhead each year.

I would be remiss if I didn't thank Mons Peak IX, Big Agnes, Outdoor Research, LEKI, Western Mountaineering, Terracea, Himali, Osprey, Peak Refuel, and Protector Brands for hooking me up with the gear used throughout this entire process. There truly is no such thing as bad weather, only bad gear. I was warm, dry, fed, and happy every night I spent on the trail.

The vast majority of the images in this book were captured by the SiOnyx Aurora Night Vision Camera. All of my climbs were tracked and shared through the Bivystick GPS system, which meant that my family and friends could follow along from home.

The family at FalconGuides gave me an incredible opportunity with this project, and I will be forever grateful that they took a chance in letting me write for them.

Spend some time acclimating to an increased elevation prior to heading up the trail. Nick Niforos is cooking up a meal outside between a Big Agnes (left) and a Mons Peak IX tent at 10,000 feet. Letting your body get used to a lower level of oxygen for a couple days before attempting to summit will reduce the chance of altitude sickness.

Almost exactly a year from standing on top of White Mountain alone, I shared the summit of Mount Shasta with a group of people I met on the way to camp at Helen Lake, and it was amazing and emotional for me as this project drew to a close. The tops of 15 mountains, each one taller than 14,000 feet, had been reached in a 12-month period by a kid from Iowa. As the sunrise bathed us on the summit, I couldn't help but think about how much this entire process has impacted my life.

The blackened and, ultimately, lost toenails to mild (if there is such a thing) frost-bite; the sunburn and dehydration; the gale-force winds, mind-numbing cold, and hip-deep snow; an earthquake or two; and a couple big ole late afternoon thunder-storms could not dampen the smallness I felt as the sun rose on Mount Whitney or the nervousness and butt-puckering feeling I had standing below the summit block of Thunderbolt. The elevation gain and loss over miles and miles of trail enhanced the experience while trying to pound my body into submission. Ask me to do it again and I will jump at the chance!

I now understand why Jack spoke so reverently and seriously about these moun-tains almost two decades ago. It takes extreme physical effort and planning to head into the backcountry with a fourteener waiting at the end of the trail. Standing on the summit is an amazing feeling. These mountains have to be treated with respect and dignity. Several people died in the Sierras in 2019 and many more had to be res-cued off the mountains. If you choose to test yourself by attempting to reach any of these summits, I hope that you find this book a good resource in the process. These mountains belong to you and me, so when you come off the trail, try to leave things better than when you got there.

Now that I have touched the top of all 15 California fourteeners to complete this book, one question still burns in my mind: How fast can I summit all of them in a row?

If, and when, that question will be answered remains to be seen.

Terms and Definitions

Altitude sickness: The negative health effect of high altitude, caused by rapid exposure to low amounts of oxygen at high elevation (typically above 8,000 feet).

Arête: A sharp mountain ridge.

Avalanche: A large mass of snow, ice, and rocks that falls down the side of a mountain.

Buttress: A projecting support of stone or brick built against a wall. Many switchback trails utilize buttresses to prevent erosion.

Cairn: A man-made pile (or stack) of stones. Cairns are used as trail markers in many parts of the world and may be painted or otherwise decorated for increased visibility. They are widely used in the Sierras to mark the trail across boulder and talus fields.

Causeway: A track, road, or railway on the upper point of an embankment across a low or wet place or piece of water, constructed of earth, masonry, wood, or concrete. Causeways are used to minimize soil erosion. There is a causeway on the way to the summit of Mount Shasta.

Chute: An inclined plane, sloping channel, or passage down or through which things may pass.

Compass: An instrument containing a magnetized pointer that shows the direction of magnetic north and bearings from it. Used with a topographic map for navigation in the backcountry.

Couloir: A steep, narrow gully on a mountainside.

Crampon: A metal plate with spikes fixed to a boot for walking on ice or rock climbing.

Crest: The top of a mountain or hill.

Crevasse: A deep open crack, especially one in a glacier.

Face: An area of vertical surface on a large rock or mountain.

Fourteener (14er): In the mountaineering parlance of the western United States, a fourteener is a mountain peak with an elevation of at least 14,000 feet (4,267 meters). Not all summits over 14,000 feet qualify as fourteeners. A rule commonly used by mountaineers in the contiguous United States is that a peak must have at least 300 feet (91 meters) of prominence to qualify. By this rule, California has 12 ranked and 3 unranked fourteeners.

Glacier: A slowly moving mass or river of ice formed by the accumulation and compaction of snow on mountains or near the poles. In California, glaciers can be found on Mount Shasta and in the Palisades throughout the year.

Glissade/glissading: The act of descending a steep snow- or scree-covered slope via a controlled slide on one's feet or buttocks. It is an alternative to other descent methods such as plunge stepping and may be used to expedite a descent or simply for the thrill.

Hypothermia: A medical emergency that occurs when your body loses heat faster than it can produce heat, causing a dangerously low body temperature. Normal body temperature is around 98.6°F (37°C); hypothermia occurs as your body temperature falls below 95°F (35°C).

Ice axe: An axe used by climbers for cutting footholds in ice, having a head with one pointed and one flattened end and a spike at the foot.

Link up: The act of connecting two things so that they can work together. To keep from going up and down one mountain after another, it is smart to link up two or more mountains. A common California fourteeners linkup combines Mount Williamson and Mount Tyndall.

Notch: An angular or V-shaped cut, indentation, or slit in an object, surface, or edge.

Pass: A navigable route through a mountain range or over a ridge.

Peak: The pointed top of a mountain.

Peak bagging: An activity in which hikers, climbers, and mountaineers attempt to reach a collection of summits, published in the form of a list.

Plate: An area of relatively level high ground.

Ridge: A long narrow hilltop, mountain range, or watershed.

Ridgeline: The topmost edge along a mountain ridge.

Rockfall: A fragment of rock (a block) that falls along a vertical or subvertical cliff and proceeds downslope by bouncing and flying along ballistic trajectories or by rolling on talus or debris slopes.

Route: A way or course taken in getting from a starting point to a destination. Often the route will be on a designated trail.

Scree: A mass of small loose stones that form or cover a slope on a mountain.

Summit: A point on a surface that is higher in elevation than all points immediately adjacent to it. The topographic terms acme, apex, peak (mountain peak), and zenith are synonymous.

Summit block: The absolute high point of a mountain.

Switchback: A trail up a steep hill or mountain that is like a zigzag pattern instead of a straight line. The zigzag pattern protects the hill and the trail from excessive erosion.

Talus: A slope formed especially by an accumulation of rock debris.

Tarn: A mountain pool that forms in a hollow scooped out by a glacier. Officially, tarns are smaller than lakes.

The trails leading to each of the summits provide an opportunity to see the mountains miles and hours before you are able to stand on top. I found that seeing the mountain from a distant approach spurred me on in anticipation. Leaving Horseshoe Meadow in the early morning hours showed me this view of Mount Langley from Hidden Lake.

Trail: A path, track, or unpaved lane or road.

Trailhead: The point at which a trail begins, where the trail is often intended for hiking, biking, horseback riding, or off-road vehicles. Modern trailheads often contain restrooms, maps, informational brochures, signposts, and parking areas for vehicles and trailers.

Traverse: To go or travel across, over, or through. On Mount Shasta, one will traverse glaciers and boulder fields.

Tree line: The edge of the habitat at which trees are capable of growing. In the Sierras, the tree line is around 10,500 feet.

Volcano: A mountain or hill, typically conical, having a crater or vent through which lava, rock fragments, hot vapor, and gas are erupting or have erupted from the earth's crust. Mount Shasta is a dormant volcano.

References

Introduction

Centers for Disease Control and Prevention. "Emergency Disinfection of Drinking Water." Last modified April 10, 2009. https://www.cdc.gov/healthywater/drinking/travel/emergency_disinfection.html.

Chapman, Gareth. "Calories Burned Hiking Calculator." Calories Burned HQ. https://caloriesburnedhq.com/calories-burned-hiking.

Engineering Toolbox. "Air Temperature and Altitude." https://www.engineeringtoolbox.com/air-altitude-temperature-d_461.html.

Felman, Adam. "What's to Know about Altitude Sickness?" *Medical News Today.* Medically reviewed on January 30, 2018. https://www.medicalnewstoday.com/articles/179819.php.

Get Bear Smart Society. "Bear Encounters." http://www.bearsmart.com/play/bear-encounters.

Mayo Clinic. "Hypothermia." March 13, 2019. https://www.mayoclinic.org/diseases-conditions/hypothermia/symptoms-causes/syc-20352682.

"Mount Whitney Lottery—Permit Reservations." USDA Forest Service, Inyo National Forest. https://www.fs.usda.gov/detail/inyo/passes-permits/recreation/?cid=stelprdb5150055.

Naismith, W. W. "Excursions: Cruach Ardran, Stobinian, and Ben More." *Scottish Mountaineering Club Journal* 2, no. 3 (September 1892): 136.

National Oceanic and Atmospheric Administration, National Weather Service. "Mountain and Valley Winds." https://www.weather.gov/safety/wind-mountain-valley.

Riebl, Shaun K., and Brenda M. Davy. "The Hydration Equation: Update on Water Balance and Cognitive Performance." ACSM's *Health & Fitness Journal* 17, no. 6 (November/December 2013): 21–28.

Seven Principles of Leave No Trace. © 1999 by the Leave No Trace Center for Outdoor Ethics. www.LNT.org.

Stump, Megan. "Hydration Basics." REI. https://www.rei.com/learn/expert-advice/hydrate.html.

Thompson, Andrea D. "Edema." *Merck Manual,* Professional Version. Last reviewed and revised June 2018. https://www.merckmanuals.com/professional/cardiovascular-disorders/symptoms-of-cardiovascular-disorders/edema.

"The Yosemite Decimal System." Climber.org. Accessed January 15, 2009. http://climber.org/data/decimal.html.

Clyde, Norman. "First Ascent of Mount Russell." *Sierra Club Bulletin*, 1927.

Farquhar, Francis P. *Place Names of the High Sierra*. 1926. Reprint, San Francisco: Sierra Club, 2007.

Inyo Independent (Independence, CA). August 17, 1871.

King, Clarence. *Mountaineering in the Sierra Nevada*. 1872. Reprint, Lincoln: University of Nebraska Press, Bison Books, 1970.

O'Rourke, Sean. *California's Fourteeners: Hikes to Climbs*. Self-published, 2017. https://drdirtbag.com/wp-content/uploads/2017/01/book-preview.pdf.

Porcella, Stephen, and Cameron Burns. *Climbing California's Fourteeners*. Rev. ed. Seattle, WA: Mountaineers Books, 2008.

Selters, Andy, and Michael Zanger. *The Mount Shasta Book*. 3rd ed. Birmingham, AL: Wilderness Press, 2006.

About the Author

Toby Evans's love of the mountains and backcountry began at age 10 during a family camping trip through Yellowstone National Park, the Tetons, and the Bitterroots. An accomplished endurance athlete and journalist, he was introduced to the California fourteeners by adventure racing teammate and former speed summit record-holder Jack McBroom. Toby has traveled, competed, climbed, and explored across the United States and internationally. His Happy Mutant Adventure Race Series has become one of the most popular events of its kind in the country. His "Fitpacking" program introduces clients to the outdoors in a logical, step-by-step manner. Evans is a certified trainer and has a master's degree in exercise science. He plans on seeing how fast all 15 summits can be reached in the future.

After a winter that left the deepest snowpack in years, hiking the "trail" to Shepards Pass meant strapping on my crampons and slogging through the snow above Mahogany Flat, making travel slow going. A late-season storm sent me back to the car without a summit. Finding a clear trail on my return in August, the travel passed rapidly and the summit was worth the wait.

A safe and successful summit trip into the Eastern Sierra back country should always end with a smile!